Pictures by Pinnacle Photo Agency

ROAD TO GLORY:
The Inside Story

by Nigel Walrond

MAIN CHIEFS SPONSOR

To my dad, John, who was
responsible for my crazy love of sport
and took me to my first Chiefs game
in the 1970s. He would be so proud
of what they have achieved.

First printed 2017

Published by Nigel Walrond

© Nigel Walrond

Printed in Great Britain by Kingfisher Print & Design, Totnes

ACKNOWLEDGEMENTS

My special thanks to Tony Rowe OBE, Rob Baxter, Tom Hayes and Dean Mumm for their contributions to the book; to Phil Mingo and Pinnacle Photo Agency for the superb pictures; to Mark Stevens, Mark Williams, Paddy Marsh, John Lockyer and Tony Walker for their invaluable assistance; to Ross Bellotti, Kim Waldron and all at Kingfisher Print and Design for all their help and hard work in putting this book together; and to my wife Jenny and our boys Luke and Joshua, for allowing me the time to do it

ISBN No: 978-1-9998360-0-9

Contents

Exeter head coach Rob Baxter and Chiefs chairman and chief executive Tony Rowe OBE hold aloft the Premiership trophy on the open-top bus parade

*Dean Mumm with the LV=
Cup he skippered Exeter to
in March 2014*

WELCOME

By Dean Mumm (Exeter Chiefs captain 2013-2015)

WHAT a pleasure it was to see Exeter Chiefs win the title.

Seven years before that, I had never heard of
the Chiefs, and Exeter for me was a place in
the southern highlands of
New South Wales, not a place in the UK

However, a game of rugby on May 27, 2017, now becomes a memory which I am unlikely to ever forget.

Sitting in my hotel room in Dunedin, New Zealand, at 1am, I quickly realised that the only way I would be able to watch the game was to stream it through my phone.

So there I was, in the early hours of the morning, lying awkwardly on my bed watching the game, tethered to the wall by the length of phone charger. Not quite as exciting as watching it from Twickenham, yet completely worth it, and as good as Steve Parrett is on *Twitter*, it's nothing compared to viewing it.

It didn't take long for the emotion of the game to take over, and by the time Steeno was lining up for the telling kicks and Simmo was wrongfully disallowed that try, I was pacing the room and blowing up at any decision that didn't go our way. Luckily, I didn't have a roomie that night.

One of the saving graces for me in that period of tension in the back end of the game (not to mention extra time!) was that I never had the feeling that the boys were going to lose.

Their sense of purpose under pressure and willingness to stick to their game was clearly evident.

Also Steeno remains the most composed and competent kicker I ever played with and he is a man that loves the moment that matters. How good that he was able to nail that moment, not once, but twice to clinch the victory for his team. How fitting then to see his hand as the equal first on the trophy.

As an outsider, one of the things so evident this year, as opposed to last year's final, was the composure shown by the entire squad when the crucial moments occurred.

Belief can be a fickle thing and doesn't happen overnight, However, significant credit needs to go to Yenz, Steeno, Rob and the coaching staff for fostering it the way that they did.

I feel that the 2017 Chiefs believed many weeks out from the final that they were more than good enough to win. The challenge was showing the rest of us and managing to do it in a style of their choosing.

I thoroughly believe that this victory was not the result of one good season. It was the culmination of a journey and the outcome of so much effort and work put in by players, past players, staff and most importantly the fans.

Consequently, the victory provided immense satisfaction to so many people and so many parties.

Rarely in sport do you see a collective of people all going in the same direction, all committed to obtaining the same goal over such a long period of time. The Chiefs as a club have this in their current culture and every single person deserves a little credit for playing his or her part.

Back in 2012, my very first game for the Chiefs was an A-League fixture against Harlequins at 'The Stoop'. An inauspicious start and we didn't manage to get the win.

However, as we rolled down the M4 on the way I was starkly aware of the quality of talent on offer at the club. The talent was yet to be polished, yet undeniable potential. There was a hint of unrefined Cornish talent with some pretty average haircuts, in the form of Nowellsy and LCD and there was a sprinkle of Devon with Yeandle, Ewers and Slade. Overwhelmingly though, there was enough talent to do something special in the years to come and I'm pleased to see the talent has matured into success.

This is one of the great elements of Rob Baxter and he deserves a lot of credit for the fortunes of the club. It is one thing to have access to talent, it is another to foster that talent and turn it into what the team needs.

Even harder is the ability to find and recruit people to the club that can enhance the quality of home-grown talent, allowing those individuals to mature and bloom. Rob has been able to achieve this and this separates him from many coaches.

Special credit also needs to go to those 'originals', the men who set the scene as the team emerged from the Championship, for creating a team culture that is honest, merit-based and sometimes amusingly ruthless. It has never allowed one individual to get bigger than the team, and it has been maintained for many years now.

Well, what a journey it has been!

Huge congratulations to Tony Rowe OBE, Rob Baxter, Jack Yeandle and Steeno and all the boys for winning the Premiership and for achieving the goal on behalf of all those with the Chiefs.

It is an absolute privilege to say that I was once a Chief and to have been involved in a chapter that promoted the success of the club.

Time to embrace the challenge of being the hunted, rather than just the hunter!

Tom Hayes returned to Sandy Park in August 2017 to play in Gareth Steenson's testimonial game, captaining the Chiefs' 2010 Championship XV to victory over a Classic Lions XV

Foreword

By Tom Hayes (Exeter Chiefs captain 2009-2013)

IT was absolutely brilliant watching Exeter Chiefs win the Premiership final against Wasps.

It was an unbelievable game, a classic final that was a real helter-skelter one, and I imagine neutrals really enjoyed it as well.

There wasn't much breathing space in it, and it was definitely edge-of-the-seat stuff.

Usually I would be fairly calm and calculated when watching a game, and it takes a lot to get me out of my chair in the sitting room, but this certainly did.

However, calling the Chiefs winning the Premiership a 'fairytale' is doing people a disservice, because it is down to a lot of hard work.

It is the result of a plan that people have been motivated to implement and drive forward, and they are now getting their just rewards.

The amount of time director of rugby Rob Baxter puts into it is just absolutely phenomenal, while chief executive Tony Rowe OBE has had his plans for a long time and has driven it on.

Some people have maybe found it hard to swallow the way he has gone about things, but looking at the bigger picture, he has done something that has clearly paid off and it is hard to argue with what he has achieved.

One of the biggest disappointments for me personally when I had to retire in 2013 through a back injury was that I knew things were still getting better.

I didn't say to myself 'I know this club is going to win the Premiership'. I didn't know where it was going to top out to be honest, but I still knew we were on the rise, so the hardest thing was to step away when I did.

How far was it going to go, I didn't know? But Tony was talking at the time that he wanted the club to be a Premiership heavy hitter and a European heavy hitter, and in fairness, that is where they are getting to, and his plan is obviously coming to fruition.

Just seeing the quality in the squad when I had to step away from it, I definitely knew there was a lot more to come.

We had already had two top-six finishes. We lost 18-15 at home to Northampton in what was effectively a quarter-final to get into the top four in the 2011-12 season, and we were maybe just a little bit green at that time, but there was definitely a top-four finish in us.

It was clear, as far as I was concerned that, just given time, the Chiefs were going to be able to get into the semi-finals, and it is no surprise it turned out that way.

Obviously at this stage, I wouldn't be playing any more, given my vintage, but I would have liked to have had another year or two with them, but it wasn't to be.

Analysing the way the Chiefs won the title, the semi-final against Saracens and the final against Wasps were both unbelievable games.

Maybe in the semi-final I thought the Chiefs were going to fall short, given how late Saracens got their try. They are able to finish teams off very late in matches, and I was thinking 'here we go again, they have backed up their European final win the previous week and they have managed to dig something out right at the death here'.

Then Henry Slade pulled that kick out and put Exeter right back in it, and Sam Simmonds got the try with the last play of the game and it was Roy of the Rovers stuff.

However, I always felt fairly confident of Exeter winning the final. They never lacked shape or composure throughout the game.

I am not saying I thought they were definitely going to win it and they had it in the bag, but they were giving as good as they were getting.

I don't think there was ever a point that either side could really feel they had it sewn up, literally until the final whistle went.

The finale to the game was incredible, and from the club's points of view, and the headline writers' point of view, having Gareth Steenson kicking the winning points couldn't have been better.

Steeno has done that so many times over the years, whether it is picking up a few points to get us a losing bonus point to get us clear of the relegation zone or helping us make the top six or top four, or getting promoted from the Championship. He has been there time and time again, and has been able to knock over some pressure kicks.

It was great that he was the man there to do it, because you know you can rely on him much more often than not.

There are not too many of the boys still knocking around now from the Championship days, but it was certainly good to still have a few of them there to show it can be done, that there is that quality playing in the Championship and fellas who can go on and play in the Premiership. I hope it will give a lot of people some realistic aspirations of what can be achieved.

When we won promotion from the Championship, my eldest child had been born in the days prior to the promotion final, so I went back to Ireland just after the game and never went out with the boys properly to celebrate our success.

I was sat there watching the celebrations at Twickenham and wishing I was over there, but unfortunately it was not to be. I would certainly have liked to have enjoyed it with them, and I have no doubt the boys did, especially after a long season when things didn't start too fantastically well for them.

But with Rob being as level-headed as he is, keeping people's feet on the ground and just keeping them as pragmatic as ever, they managed to turn things around and just started getting the results when it mattered.

I remember Leicester, going back a few years, timing their run well towards the end of the season and coming from a fairly lowly position a couple of times and finishing up as champions, and I am fairly sure Wasps did as well.

I would imagine Rob kept his composure and obviously didn't lose his way at all when things weren't going fantastically well in that patch at the start of the season, and it ended up with the team going on a record-breaking run for the club.

It was wonderful to see and a great reward for everyone involved at Sandy Park.

Tom Hayes celebrates Exeter's Championship-winning success on the open-top bus parade in May 2010

Jack Nowell lifts the Aviva Premiership trophy high above his head at Twickenham

CHAPTER 1

ROAD TO GLORY:
The Inside Story

WE are living in strange times, where we have come to expect the unexpected.

The United Kingdom voting to leave the European Union; Prime Minister Theresa May failing to get a House of Commons majority in the General Election after pundits had initially predicted a landslide victory for the Conservatives; Donald Trump stunning the world by winning the United States of America presidential election; and Leicester City Football Club lifting the Premier League trophy.

To that list we can surely add Exeter Chiefs capturing the Premiership title after only seven years in the top flight.

Admittedly, it does not register as high on the Richter scale as some of those aforementioned events.

After all, Exeter reached the Twickenham final in 2016, only losing to European champions Saracens by eight points, having spent most of that season in the top four, and for a large part of it, the top two.

Their place among English rugby's elite clubs had become widely accepted, so it should therefore have come as little surprise to see them back at English rugby headquarters 12 months later.

However, beating Wasps, who led the Premiership table for most of the 2016-17 season, was still deemed a remarkable achievement, and quite rightly so.

Excellent *BT Sport* commentator Nick Mullins summed it up best as the Chiefs lifted the Premiership trophy.

"From Little Chiefs to Big Chiefs to champions," exclaimed Mullins.

"Incredibly, wonderfully, magically…. it is Exeter."

The way the Chiefs claimed the Premiership crown, after making such an indifferent start to the season, is one of the reasons why their success is such an incredible tale.

When England winger Semesa Rokoduguni brushed past a couple of weak tackles in the eighth minute of injury time to snatch a 13-10 victory for Bath over their West Country rivals at Sandy Park on October 30, a top-six finish and a place in the following season's European Champions Cup looked to be Exeter's best hope of salvaging something from what looked like being a disappointing campaign.

They had only won two of their opening seven Premiership games and seemed to be suffering from the mother of all Twickenham hangovers.

If anyone had said then that the Bath game would be the last time the Chiefs would taste defeat in the league during the season, men in white coats would most definitely have been summoned.

Instead, that is exactly what happened, with Exeter winning 15 and drawing two of their remaining 17 matches, tying the Premiership record for most games unbeaten set by the great Leicester Tigers team of the 1999-2000 season featuring the likes of Martin Johnson and Neil Back as they lifted the second of four successive league titles before a play-off final was introduced.

Top: Exeter Chiefs Supporters Club chairman Richard Cresswell (centre) leads the drumming at Twickenham
Bottom: Exeter Chiefs fans celebrate their success in the Premiership final
Bottom right : Rob Baxter with the Premiership trophy in the Twickenham dressing room

The Chiefs also set Premiership records for the most successive bonus-point victories (eight), and for picking up a try-scoring bonus point in nine consecutive league games.

But, despite all of that, it is their amazing rise over the past decade or so that makes Exeter's achievement so fascinating and compelling to the wider public, both in Devon and across the UK, even to those who have little interest in rugby union.

I received messages from *BBC Radio Devon* listeners after the Twickenham final saying they had no interest in the sport at all, but they just could not bring themselves to turn the radio off as those exciting, tension-filled moments ticked away, firstly at the end of the normal 80 minutes, and then extra time.

It is why Exeter have been widely regarded as everyone's second favourite team during their time in the Premiership (though that is something that might now change after their Twickenham success!).

Tony Rowe OBE and his fellow directors dared to dream more than a decade ago, and there is nothing that people love more than a fairytale ending.

From a mudheap at the old, though still fondly remembered by many, County Ground, where rugby was watched by just several hundred people, to a superb, purpose-built stadium beside the M5 motorway with a capacity now standing at over 13,000.

From playing the likes of Pertemps Bees (Birmingham-Solihull), Otley and Sedgley Park only a decade ago to now finishing ahead of some of the great names in English rugby, such as Bath, Leicester Tigers, Wasps, Harlequins and Northampton Saints.

Exeter have shown what can be achieved with the right vision and planning, spot-on decision-making, clever appointments, great coaching and shrewd on-the-field recruitment.

They never tried to run before they could walk, taking small steps along the Road to Glory, building each season and learning from any mistakes they made.

They have given hope to every club in England with ambitions to one day make it big and have provided the template for possible success.

The Chiefs' case study has also added considerable strength to the argument of those fervently against ring-fencing, and who are desperate to keep the route into the Premiership open to everyone.

This is the fascinating inside story, largely through the eyes of Rob Baxter – who was head coach for the 2016-17 season but has since been handed the title of director of rugby – of how Exeter Chiefs pulled off arguably the most incredible team sporting achievement the South West has ever seen.

Rob Baxter in full cry during the warm-up for the pre-season game with Scarlets at Sandy Park

CHAPTER 2

Pre-season Doubts

EVERYTHING looked so good for Exeter Chiefs at the start of the 2016-17 season.

They had kept their Twickenham-reaching squad together and had made three excellent signings to add to it, in the shape of Bath and England centre Ollie Devoto and Australian international duo Dave Dennis and Greg Holmes.

They had come through three pre-season friendlies in impressive style, seeing off Pro12 sides Scarlets (45-3) and Ulster (25-19) at Sandy Park, and rounding off their warm-up games with a Friday night victory at Newport-Gwent Dragons (32-16).

I had said, live on *BBC Radio Devon*, within minutes of the Chiefs losing in the final to Saracens that I expected both teams to be back at Twickenham 12 months later, and on the eve of the season, that remained my unshakeable belief.

However, even at that stage, Exeter head coach Rob Baxter was having some doubts.

In hindsight, he realised it all stemmed from how he had reacted to that defeat at Twickenham some three months before.

That was perhaps borne out of eagerness to avoid what had happened to Bath, who lost the 2015 final to Saracens and had backed that up with a disastrous ninth-place finish in the Premiership table the following campaign by maybe having massive doubts over what they were doing, rather than appreciating they were a very good team.

"I remember talking to the players in the dressing room after the Saracens game, and my over-riding feeling was to make sure that the players appreciated what a good season they had experienced," said Baxter.

"Looking back on it, maybe that was a little bit of an incorrect way to deal with the day, but it did feel like the right thing to say at that time.

"We had just had our best ever season. We had never been in the top four before, let alone getting a home semi-final and winning that, and then getting to Twickenham.

"Because we have all massively driven the positives at the club year on year for a long time, and that has been one of the things that has been a foundation for us, in terms of how we are going to get better, how we are going to improve and the things we are doing, I didn't want the season to pass away without stopping and saying 'we have done well'.

"That was how I felt on the day, and to be honest, I didn't feel we got too much wrong after that, and we obviously didn't get too much wrong because the squad of players we had together for the next season was good – and of course, we ultimately went on to win the Premiership with it – so a lot of what we had in place was really good.

"But, as a coaching group, and we have talked about this amongst ourselves, we probably made a few mistakes in that our approach is very much about how we can get better, and what can we do to improve? And we probably looked at it in a bit too much detail.

"If you look at the areas that each of us was responsible for – Rob Hunter with the forwards and the set piece, myself with the defence and Ali Hepher with the attack – we probably over-analysed how we wanted to improve.

"As a coaching unit we obviously wanted to be better, we wanted to win more games and win the Premiership and do well in Europe, but I think maybe we looked at some of the things we probably felt we were doing wrong, and over-focused on the mistakes we made and how we would try to rectify those.

"In hindsight, we learnt that what we needed to focus on were a lot of the positives, the really good things that got us to the final and the really good strengths we had.

"If you look at teams who have built successful seasons on the back of successful seasons, they get better at what they are good at, and Saracens and Leicester Tigers are great examples of that.

"Saracens have been hugely about the quality of their defence and their press, and that overall pressure game they put you under with their set piece, and their tactical awareness in the territorial battle.

"They are a really good example of a team who have not always won finals and semi-finals, but what they have improved is some of their strengths.

"After Twickenham, we over-focused on a few things that had been our weaknesses."

Exeter had boasted one of the best defences in the Premiership in the 2015-16 season, but Baxter returned to the club early from his summer break to go through videos of the previous campaign's games to try and find a way to make it even better.

"Defensively, I looked in detail at how we had conceded every try through the Premiership season," he explained.

"We conceded quite a lot of tries with changes in direction and on blindside attacks, and we probably over-focused on that, and actually we had one of the best defences in the Premiership over the 22 games, and what had created that was our line speed, our enthusiasm to go forward and tackle, and our energy and our kick chase.

"All the things that were real qualities, I don't think we assumed they'd be there because we talked about them and pointed them out as highlights for us, but our focus and our work went into trying to defend situations that happen relatively rarely in a match, and don't often cost you a game, and it wasn't those situations that had cost us the final.

"In the set piece, there were a couple of changes last summer about how a maul was to be formed, how scrums were to be refereed and that we would have to play the ball away from scrums a lot more and very quickly, but actually it didn't really materialise like that over the season.

"Sometimes you do get told to play the ball away from a scrum, but actually, if you get a good, dominant, go-forward scrummage, as the final against Wasps showed, you can still use it as a real weapon, as can be the maul.

"I think we over-focused on the fact the ball was going to be produced from line-outs and scrums a lot more, whereas actually what was important was producing really tidy, good-quality possession.

"Going forward in a maul and going forward as a scrum, going forward in defence, kick-chasing absolutely flat out – those are all massive attitude battles – and though we felt those were in our DNA and those things would be there, we probably didn't talk about them enough and drive them enough through training."

So how did the Exeter head coach feel going into the new campaign?

"I felt pretty good. I was disappointed we had lost the final, but the overall emotion was we were still on an upward curve.

"However, looking back now, I can see what we got wrong a little bit.

"We shouldn't have really looked at it being a successful season, as much as it was. We probably should have talked a little bit about the fact it was hurting us to lose that game to Saracens, maybe even straight after the final, and what were we going to do about it to win the next final?

"I still look back and ask myself whether I could have said that in the dressing room after the game, and I don't know if I could.

"Because we had reached our first Premiership final and had enjoyed such a good season, I don't really know how I could have stood there before that group of players and said to them: 'This isn't good enough lads. I want to see a group of players that are going to do something about this'.

"I just don't know if it would have worked then, and what the impact of that would have been on them.

"As it turned out, we realised that was the case after a few weeks of the season, and we confronted it head on and it obviously had a huge bearing."

With their campaign not finishing until May 27 due to the final, the likes of Jack Nowell, Henry Slade, Luke Cowan-Dickie, Don Armand, Alec Hepburn, Sam Hill, Mitch Lees, Dave Ewers, Ollie Devoto, Michele Campagnaro, Tomas Francis and Elvis Taione all away on international duty in the early part of the summer and therefore late back for pre-season, and new signing Dave Dennis not arriving at the club until early August after the conclusion of the Super Rugby season with New South Wales Waratahs, the Chiefs did not have the perfect pre-season.

"The boys came in and trained well," explained Baxter. "We didn't have any issues with the players.

"One thing that upset me a little bit in the early part of the season is that quite a few people from the outside were assuming there was an issue at the club – but there wasn't.

"We didn't have any problem players, we didn't have players turning up late, we didn't have players thinking they were absolute world beaters, we didn't have players thinking they were fantastic and showing a bad attitude. There wasn't any of that. The guys came in and trained hard.

There is no rugby pressure put on them, it is just about building friendships and getting to know each other. . .

"We were a little bit down on our previous fitness scores, but we had our shortest pre-season ever. We had guys playing right up until the end of May, which we had never had before, and you have got to give them a mandatory break, and we also had an England Saxons tour alongside an England tour that we had an unprecedented amount of people involved with (it included Ali Hepher as Saxons head coach and Robbie Beddard as strength and conditioning coach).

"Then you add in guys being away with Wales, Italy and Tonga, and you start to think 'we have got a lot of players missing here'.

"Those guys came back to us at regular intervals through pre-season training, so we ended up with an even shorter amount of pre-season, so we had more disruptions and issues in our pre-season than we had ever had before, but I never felt we weren't training well or hard."

An example of the disruption the international matches caused was summed up by the club's annual pre-season team-bonding trip to Portugal.

"We always have a two-day trip away at the start of pre-season, where the squad go and just have a good time," explained Baxter.

"There is no rugby pressure put on them, it is just about building friendships and getting to know each other, and just spending 48 hours in each other's company in a nice environment.

Top: Club stalwart Matt Jess on his way against Scarlets to what would be his last first-team try for the Chiefs before leaving the playing staff

Middle: New Exeter Chiefs signing from Bath, centre Ollie Devoto, making his debut in the pre-season friendly against Ulster

Bottom right: Dave Dennis, another one of Chiefs' summer signings, in typical action on his debut against Ulster

Bottom left: Olly Woodburn scores one of his three tries against Dragons, making it five in three pre-season games for the on-fire winger

Inset: Exeter head coach Rob Baxter sensing at Rodney Parade that something was not quite right with his side

"I remember it didn't feel like a team getting ready for a big season.

"In a way we had a group of players back together who were almost celebrating what the season before had been about.

"All of our England Saxons and full internationals turned up at the club and it was the first thing that they did. The likes of Cowan-Dickie, Nowellsy and Sladey were getting off a plane from Australia, and their first involvement with the club was to literally get back on a plane and go off on a two-day party really.

"Their season had just finished, and they were not thinking about the following season. They were thinking about playing in a Premiership final and being on an England tour to Australia.

"All of a sudden you have got 10 to 12 players there who are still tied up in the season that has just happened, and because of the short pre-season, we hadn't factored in getting the lads back in for two or three days of pre-season before we went away.

"When I look back, that was two days really based around having a good time because we had enjoyed a good season, and not really based around what was coming.

"So this year, after winning the final, we had them in for two days of training before we went away, and even though it trimmed our off-season break by a couple of days, I think it was really valuable because it let us set the scene and set the stall out for where we want to go now."

Despite the disjointed summer, Exeter enjoyed three good pre-season wins over Scarlets, Ulster and Newport-Gwent Dragons – always a confidence boost going into a fresh campaign.

"Our three pre-season games were all decent results. It wasn't the strongest Scarlets team for our first game, but it was still pretty good and we won by 40 points," said Baxter.

"It was a decent Ulster team that came to us, and when you think they scored two tries in the last ten minutes, that was a pretty comfortable and comprehensive victory for us.

"We then went to Newport-Gwent Dragons, and I have to admit, looking back on it, that was the game where I felt 'this doesn't feel quite right'.

"It took us a while to really win the game. The Dragons came at us like they were relishing playing an English team who had just been in a Premiership final, and they caused us some issues.

"I am not saying it rattled us, but it took us a while to find a way to win that game, and that was probably for me when the alarm bells started to ring a little bit."

PRE-SEASON FRIENDLIES

EXETER CHIEFS 45 SCARLETS 3
(Saturday, August 13, Sandy Park)

Chiefs: L Turner (O Woodburn ht); M Bodilly (L Turner 62), I Whitten (P Laverick ht), T Hendrickson (S Hill ht), J Short (M Jess ht); W Hooley (J Simmonds 9, G Steenson ht), S Townsend (J Maunder ht); C Rimmer (B Moon ht), J Yeandle (S Malton ht), H Williams (M Low ht); J Hill (O Atkins ht), D Welch (G Parling ht); D Ewers (T Johnson ht), S Simmonds (J Salvi ht), K Horstmann (T Waldrom ht).

Scarlets: A Thomas (R Smith ht); I Nicholas, S Hughes, H Parkes (capt), S Evans; R Patchell (D Jones ht, A Thomas 62), J Evans (D Smith 73); D Evans (W Jones ht), R Elias (T Davies ht, D Hughes 73), P Edwards (W Taylor 28, W Kruger 53); R Bernardo (T Beirne ht), T Price (D Bulbring 36); A Shingler (L Rawlins ht), W Boyde (J McLeod 62), M Allen (T Phillips 57).

Chiefs: Tries – Williams, Johnson, Woodburn (2), Jess, Waldrom; Conversions – J Simmonds, Steenson (5); Penalty – Hooley. **Scarlets:** Penalty – Patchell.

Yellow Card: Scarlets – Beirne.

HT: 10-3. **Referee:** Tom Foley (RFU). **Attendance:** 4,940.

EXETER CHIEFS 25 ULSTER 19
(Saturday, August 20, Sandy Park)

Chiefs: L Turner (P Dollman ht); O Woodburn (M Jess ht), M Bodilly (J Short ht), S Hill (O Devoto ht), I Whitten (M Bodilly 60); G Steenson (capt, H Slade ht), W Chudley (D Lewis ht); A Hepburn (M Low 60), L Cowan-Dickie (E Taione 60), T Francis (G Holmes 49); M Lees (O Atkins 60), D Welch (G Parling 60); D Ewers (D Dennis 46), J Salvi (B White 60), D Armand (T Waldrom 60).

Ulster: C Piutau (S Windsor 65); L Ludik, D Cave (D Busby 65), S McCloskey, J Stockdale (R Lyttle 69); B Herron (J McPhillips 59), R Pienaar (P Marshall ht); C Black (A Warwick 30), R Herring (capt, J Andrew 59), R Ah You (J Simpson 49, K McCall 55); P Browne (K Treadwell 49), F Van Der Merwe (A O'Connor 58); R Diack (S Mulholland 60), C Ross, R Wilson (M Rea 51).

Chiefs: Tries – Armand, Chudley, Welch, penalty try; Conversion – Slade; Penalty – Slade. **Ulster:** Tries – Stockdale, Lyttle (2); Conversions – Pienaar, McPhillips.

HT: 10-7. **Referee:** Greg Macdonald (RFU). **Attendance:** 6,429.

NEWPORT-GWENT DRAGONS 16 EXETER CHIEFS 32
(Friday, August 26, Rodney Parade)

Dragons: C Meyer; (G Gasson 73) A Warren, S Beard (G Rhys Jones 73), J Dixon (C Davies 78), P Howard; N Macleod (A O'Brien 64), S Pretorious (L Jones 69); S Hobbs (T Davies ht), T Rhys Thomas (capt, R Buckley 58), C Mitchell (L Fairbrother ht); M Screech (N Crosswell ht-44, A Sweet 55), C Hill; O Griffiths, N Cudd, E Jackson (H Keddie 64). Replacement (not used): D Harris.

Chiefs: P Dollman (L Turner 72); O Woodburn (W Hooley 78), O Devoto (M Bodilly 75), S Hill (G Steenson 55), I Whitten (J Short 62); H Slade, W Chudley (D Lewis 62); B Moon (A Hepburn 55), L Cowan-Dickie (J Yeandle 62), H Williams (G Holmes 58); M Lees (G Parling 55), D Welch; D Armand (capt), J Salvi (T Waldrom 69), T Waldrom (D Dennis 62).

Dragons: Try – Howard; Conversion – Macleod; Penalties – Meyer, Macleod (2). **Chiefs:** Tries – Woodburn (3), Cowan-Dickie, Devoto; Conversions – Slade, Steenson; Penalty – Slade.

HT: 13-13. **Referee:** Nigel Owens (Wales). **Attendance:** 3,384.

Luke Cowan-Dickie is tackled by Gloucester duo David Halaifonua and Ben Morgan

CHAPTER 3

Sticky Start

PREMIERSHIP TABLE							
	P	W	D	L	F	A	Pts
Saracens	6	5	0	1	175	59	25
Wasps	6	5	0	1	210	127	23
Bath	6	5	0	1	172	84	22
Leicester	6	4	0	2	172	139	19
EXETER	**6**	**2**	**1**	**3**	**156**	**148**	**15**
Newcastle	6	3	0	3	83	127	14
Sale	6	2	1	3	120	149	13
Harlequins	6	3	0	3	111	140	12
Northampton	6	2	0	4	102	114	11
Gloucester	6	1	2	3	126	134	11
Worcester	6	1	2	3	106	172	9
Bristol	6	0	0	6	82	222	2

SEPTEMBER

Sunday 4	AP	L	Wasps 25	Exeter Chiefs 20
Sunday 11	AP	L	Exeter Chiefs 13	Saracens 34
Saturday 17	AP	W	Exeter Chiefs 36	Harlequins 25
Friday 23	AP	W	Bristol 17	Exeter Chiefs 41
Friday 30	AP	L	Northampton Saints 20	Exeter Chiefs 19

OCTOBER

Saturday 8	AP	D	Exeter Chiefs 27	Gloucester 27

Premiership points available 30 – points taken 15

(AP = Aviva Premiership, AWC = Anglo-Welsh Cup; ECC = European Champions Cup)

IF alarm bells were already ringing with Rob Baxter after that Dragons game, they must have been partly silenced by Exeter's first-half display in their eagerly-awaited Premiership opener at Wasps, as they led 17-8 at the interval.

Someone with a warped sense of humour had handed the Chiefs two of the toughest fixtures imaginable to start their campaign – against the two sides with which they had ended the previous season.

A Ricoh Arena clash with a Wasps side who Exeter had beaten in the Premiership semi-final back in May but who were now being tipped by many to win the Premiership in 2017 after the sprinkling of some considerable stardust over the club in the summer in the form of Australian international Kurtley Beale, South African ace Willie Le Roux (who did not arrive at the club until February), Bath centre Kyle Eastmond and enigmatic, and often controversial, former England fly-half Danny Cipriani.

And that was followed a week later by a Sabbath Day match with reigning Premiership and European champions Saracens at Sandy Park, less than four months since they had locked horns at Twickenham.

Before a ball had been kicked, I had tipped Wasps to just miss out on a top-four finish in the league as I felt there were too many big personalities at the club to provide the right dressing-room mix, and that they would fade away after a good start to the campaign. How wrong was I?!

Injuries denied them the services of Beale, Eastmond and England flanker James Haskell for the Chiefs opener, but they gave debuts to Cipriani and his former Sale Sharks team-mate Tommy Taylor.

Exeter, meanwhile, kept faith with 11 of the starting line-up that had lost to Saracens at Twickenham, with Jack Nowell still recovering from surgery on a broken thumb and the very unlucky Dave Ewers again sidelined with a knee ligament injury that would ultimately keep him out until early November, having missed three months of the previous campaign with a similar problem.

There was a Premiership debut for Ollie Devoto at outside centre after his move from Bath, while fellow newcomers Greg Holmes and Dave Dennis were on the bench.

The huge talking point, though, was the selection of Henry Slade at fly-half, with the Premiership's 2015-16 Golden Boot winner with 258 points, Gareth Steenson, left kicking his heels on the bench alongside club skipper Jack Yeandle, which meant Don Armand was entrusted with the captaincy.

Henry Slade was a surprise selection at fly-half for the opening game of the season at Wasps

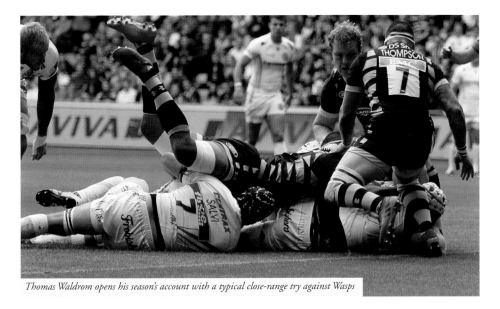

Thomas Waldrom opens his season's account with a typical close-range try against Wasps

Wasps had won their last nine matches at the Ricoh Arena in all competitions, but had lost their league opener in each of the previous four seasons.

The rolling maul that had caused Wasps so much grief the previous season got the Chiefs off to a fine start, with who else but No.8 Thomas Waldrom dotting down, as he looked to surpass his previous season's tally of 13 touchdowns that had seen him crowned as the Premiership's Top Try Scorer.

Class act Jimmy Gopperth, the Kiwi fly-half who always seemed to save his best for matches against Exeter, stood Chiefs winger Olly Woodburn up to cross in the corner and finish off a slick handling move to get Wasps' first of 84 league tries in the season.

But Exeter finished the half strongly, with some wonderful touchline interplay between Sam Hill and Will Chudley serving up a try for the latter, with Slade adding his second conversion of the game for a nine-point half-time lead.

The Chiefs dominated the opening ten minutes of the second half, but their only reward was a Slade penalty due to some excellent home defending.

The momentum of the game suddenly changed, with Christian Wade's right-touchline break creating a three-on-one situation that provided a converted try for Dan Robson, but some fine Chiefs defence, including a thumping hit by Alec Hepburn on Taylor, denied them a second score until just past the hour mark, when Taylor rounded off a driving maul, and Gopperth's conversion put them ahead for the first time in the game at 22-20.

Slade missed with a long-range penalty attempt, before Gopperth safely dispatched another three-pointer of his own late on to seal victory.

It was a game that gave Baxter plenty of food for thought, and whereas most Exeter fans would have probably settled for a losing bonus point before the contest, he was far from satisfied.

"We led for a large part of the game before losing it late on, so what was the right reaction to it?" said Baxter.

"You know Wasps are a good team, they were a top-four side the previous season, they are at home, they have had a decent pre-season and have got a lot of good players, so a bonus point away from home in the Premiership against one of the top-four sides is not too bad.

"That is kind of how you want to talk because, in coaching, you never want to get into panic mode after one loss, and we never have here at Exeter, so there was no panic, but I think that was when we started to feel things were not quite right.

"It is a big thing, over a period of time, to talk about the feel of things.

"When you sit down as a coaching group – I have spent a lot of time with Ali Hepher, and I am spending more time with Rob Hunter now and a lot of time with Ricky Pellow – you can sometimes say after a game 'that felt a bit off' or 'I didn't think that was very good', but when you analyse the game and look at the stats and break things down, you actual realise you have seen one or two things that have clouded your judgement and you are not quite right.

"Even though we did start to feel like it wasn't quite where we wanted it to be, there were a lot of reasons for that.

"We knew we'd had the shortest pre-season, we knew we hadn't quite got everyone back up and running, and we had still gone away and performed quite well.

"We therefore took the approach to not panic into changing things and thinking there were loads of issues to put right, when actually there might not be.

"We had won our three pre-season games and we had now lost against one of the best sides in the Premiership, and that was very much how we spoke at that time."

Below: *Saracens scrum-half Richard Wigglesworth was yellow carded for this ugly trip on Henry Slade*

Right: *All in a day's work for a bloodied Dave Dennis against Saracens*

sw comms

If anyone was going to expose any potential shortcomings at that stage, it was going to be Saracens, who turned up at Sandy Park off the back of a 35-3 hammering of Worcester at Twickenham the previous weekend.

England fly-half Owen Farrell was rested due to a slight back strain, but his replacement Alex Lozowski showed why he was one of the main talking points in the opening weeks of the new Premiership season with a very assured display in the number 10 shirt.

He relished playing behind a pack of forwards that included all of Sarries' stars, such as Mako and Billy Vunipola, Jamie George, Maro Itoje and Schalk Burger, though George Kruis was forced to drop out just before kick-off with a back spasm, and the Londoners stormed to a five-try victory in a dominant display in front of watching England head coach Eddie Jones.

Scotland international winger Sean Maitland helped himself to two tries, Lozowski capitalised on some lacklustre tackling to ghost through the Exeter defence, and Jackson Wray and former Ivybridge Community College student Ben Spencer also crossed, while Alex Goode was on kicking duties.

Exeter's only consolation was a Luke Cowan-Dickie try.

There was an eerie silence around the ground as Spencer picked off a loose Slade pass in time-added-on to race in unopposed for the last try, as the Exeter fans tried to come to terms with the fact that the gap between their side and the reigning champions had appeared to have grown massively in only four months.

"We then lost our second game, when we were well beaten by Saracens, but again you could say, they are English champions, they have dealt with these kinds of seasons before and know what they are doing, but in a way, losing 13-34 should be sounding some alarm bells," said Baxter.

There is nothing Harlequins' Luke Wallace can do to stop Luke Cowan-Dickie getting his first try on his way to a hat-trick

"I was then starting to get a little bit edgy, although it was a really tough start for us, and if you chuck in Harlequins at home as our next game as well, we probably had three games tougher than anybody else had at the beginning of the season.

"There is always a reason to keep moving forward and keep saying 'we will be okay'."

Despite being able to explain away those opening two defeats, due to the quality of the opposition, the Premiership table made very grim reading.

Exeter were at the foot of the pile, even below Bristol, with only one point to their name and already nine behind leaders Saracens, and although it was very early days, it was very hard to take in, especially after the previous season's success.

"It is difficult to see yourself at the bottom when you have been in the top two the previous season, and especially when we have always really targeted getting out of the blocks and starting well," said Baxter.

"I like doing that because it takes a bit of pressure off you. It lets you talk about resting the odd player, or looking after guys who might be risking a niggling injury, and it allows you to keep talking in a very positive and progressive way.

"However, the danger for us was that we could look at it by saying we had lost both games but they had been to Wasps and Saracens, and in a funny kind of way that hurt us a little bit because, I know it sounds a bit odd now but, it was kind of okay to lose those two games.

"We were bottom of the table, but you could say: 'Were we that bad at Wasps?' We were leading for most of the game and we conceded a bit of a soft try through Jimmy Gopperth that still haunts me now and I still can't really work out how we didn't tackle him.

England and British and Irish Lions past and present, as Geoff Parling contests a line-out with Saracens' Maro Itoje

Tomas Francis is red carded against Harlequins by referee Matt Carley in front of Chiefs skipper Gareth Steenson

Olly Woodburn, scoring his third try in two games in the match at Northampton, was delighting Rob Baxter with his performances

"We ran out of steam a little bit at the end, but I think Wasps were really hurt by being knocked out in the semi-finals and had enjoyed a really good pre-season, whereas we'd had a shorter pre-season and we were probably a little bit off physically and paid for that a bit in the latter stages of the game.

"You can excuse it away, and then the week after we had Saracens, and you could find what sound like excuses for that defeat as well, but some of them were genuine reasons, and because of that I wasn't panicking as we had just played the two strongest teams in the Premiership.

"It was a slow process from that last pre-season game at Newport that it was starting to feel not quite right.

"I couldn't put my finger on anything. I couldn't pick you out a stat, a score, a moment or individual performance that made me feel like that. You just start to get that inkling that 'are we just waiting for the season to ignite and take off?'"

With rugby pundits across the whole media spectrum, like Baxter, also unable to put their finger on what was going wrong for the Chiefs, the unfortunate Slade became an easy scapegoat.

Slade picked at fly-half rather than centre, Steenson is on the bench, and Exeter are not firing properly – that must be the reason for all of their early-season woes!

That was grossly unfair on the hugely talented young man because, even though he did not have his best two games against Wasps and Saracens, they were not his worst either.

That said, I must admit I was more than a bit baffled over the decision to leave Steenson on the bench and have Slade at 10, and so were many of the club's supporters.

The whole situation was not helped by the fact that, as soon as Steenson was restored to his usual position, and Slade moved out to inside centre for the visit of Harlequins in game three, Exeter returned to winning ways with a 36-25 victory. Slade had his best game of the campaign so far and all was now right with the world, or so the pundits would have you believe.

Looking back at that tricky period where the midfield make-up of his team became the topic of every interview he did, Baxter said: "Henry started those first couple of games at 10 and suffered from an under-performing team.

"It was a one to 15 under-performance, not horrifically so, because we could have won at Wasps, but we brought Steeno back in because I thought he would just be a little bit more vocal and possibly give us a little bit more direction when we started to need to drive things a little bit.

"Henry is a young player who was not only out there trying to win games when they are not going your way, but also trying to win games for a team that was in the Premiership final the season before.

"It wasn't like we were a team who had under-performed the previous year and had finished in the bottom three or bottom half, and you opt for a fresh start and the pressure is off him a little bit and he has got a bit of time to work his way into it.

"The pressure of being in the final the year before was probably all part of it, and all part of people around him not talking as much as they needed to, so he didn't talk as much as he needed to, and that's what I felt, and I think Ali was the same. It was just about, over a period of a few weeks, simplifying things a bit, getting a little bit more direction and vocality into it, and getting more players out there that were going to talk.

"Let's not forget, during a large part of the previous season we had played Henry in the midfield, so it wasn't that we felt he didn't have a place out there on the pitch. It was about finding the combination that was going to move us through this transition period from being okay to becoming high performing, and Henry played a large part in that.

"That is the bit that people don't always appreciate. They think it was a Steeno or Henry situation, but actually, what it came down to was Steeno and Henry, compared to just Henry.

"Starting Henry at 12 also changed our bench options, because you don't have to carry a 10 on your bench and you have got more impact from there.

"There were all types of things that worked in that transition period we were going through.

"I don't need to make any excuses for it. We got the group of players on the field that we wanted to have out there. It sounds very simplistic, but a lot of times it is.

"Sometimes people can really complicate selection, and often it isn't."

Baxter admitted the decision to start the season with Slade at fly-half was partly borne out of the close-season analysis, referred to before, by the coaching staff as they sought potential ways to improve the team and turn them into a title-winning side.

"Everyone is aware that Henry is a guy with a lot of potential, and what has to be remembered is that, we had a good season in 2015-16 but we didn't win the final," he said.

"My role as head coach is to try and find ways of progressing and moving forward, and some of those will be based around personnel, and some will be based around the way we play.

"Did we get all of those decisions right? Well, obviously, there were things not right at the start of the season, and some of them will be down to how we potentially asked Henry and the team to play, and some of them will be down to personnel, and some will be down to how each individual played.

"It is too simplistic to say that was the way we thought the team was going to move forward. It was one of several things we thought, and the season showed that that wasn't necessarily the case."

That first win of the season for Exeter, against Harlequins, came as a great relief to everyone, and it was much more like what the Chiefs' supporters had come to expect from their side, especially at home, where they had not lost successive matches since September 2014.

Full-back Phil Dollman was sidelined through a broken hand, so Lachie Turner switched from wing to the No.15 shirt, and it was a position he revelled in as he bagged a couple of tries in the game.

He was outdone through by Cowan-Dickie, who must have impressed watching England forwards coach Neal Hatley with a hat-trick of tries in an outstanding, ubiquitous display by the Cornish-born hooker and product of the Chiefs' Academy set-up.

Exeter had their worries early on, as they trailed 6-5 to two Tim Swiel penalties, after taking the lead with a seventh-minute Turner touchdown.

Cowan-Dickie was gifted his first try when Quins overthrew their own line-out five metres from their line, and that was soon followed by one of the tries of the season.

Breaking off a scrum deep inside their own half, the ball was moved swiftly from left to right to give Woodburn the space to charge downfield and deliver a sumptuous back-of-the-hand offload to Turner, who raced in unopposed.

Lachie Turner scores a glorious try, his second of the match against Harlequins, after a sumptuous offload by Olly Woodburn

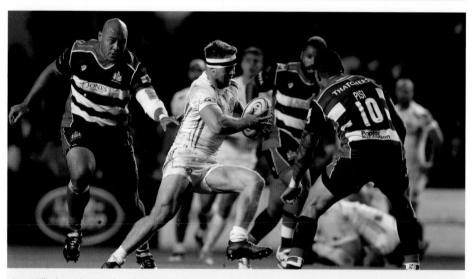

Sam Hill sidesteps his way through the Bristol defence for a splendid fifth try of the game for Exeter

Hooker Rob Buchanan responded by being driven over for a score, but Exeter had the game firmly in their grasp early in the second half, with a Cowan-Dickie try off a driving maul either side of half-time putting them 36-13 in front.

Quins, who were without star injured duo Nick Evans and Jamie Roberts for the game, came storming back with touchdowns from Danny Care and Charlie Walker, but referee Matt Carley had spotted an indiscretion in the lead-up to that second score, and after reviewing footage with TMO David Sainsbury, Exeter prop Tomas Francis was red carded after accidentally making contact with Care's head with his shin as he tried to kick the ball out of a ruck.

It seemed an incredibly harsh decision, but correct by the letter of the law, and it left Exeter having to survive a very nervy last 10 minutes, but they did so without further damage and everything suddenly looked a whole lot brighter in Chiefs World.

Next up was number one of six Friday night trips during the Premiership season for Exeter, as they visited Bristol's newly-refurbished Ashton Gate home for the first time.

It was also the first occasion the two sides had met competitively since that fabulous night at the Memorial Stadium in May 2010, when Exeter won the second leg of the Championship final 29-10 to reach the Premiership for the first time in their history with a 38-16 aggregate success.

There were just two survivors from that magical night on show – one for each side – with Gareth Steenson for Exeter and former Chiefs lock James Phillips for Bristol.

Chiefs were without the injured Armand and suspended Francis, but Dave Dennis made his first start for the club.

It might have been the shortest away trip of the season, but it became one of the most difficult, with an accident on the M5 causing major delays and persuading some fans to return home.

I made it to my commentary seat with seconds to spare before the start of the game, and the supporters' coach was also close to missing the kick-off.

It was just as well they did get there in time, otherwise they would have missed the first try of the game, after only two minutes from Woodburn, which must have left Bristol fans fearing the worst after their crushing 70-22 defeat at Wasps the weekend before.

The former Bath flyer went on to add another, with Slade having an important hand in both scores with some wonderful passing, and Woodburn's brace was matched by two close-range efforts from Waldrom, while Sam Hill – who had created Woodburn's second try with a neat offload – showed some excellent footwork to go over near the end for try number five after a superb pass off the deck by Dennis.

Steenson once again showed his obvious liking for heaping misery on Bristol with a 100 per cent record with his boot, slotting five conversions and two penalties for a personal 16-point haul.

In stark contrast, his opposite number, Samoan Tusi Pisi, had a shocker, but Bristol did score three tries, through Jordan Williams, Ross McMillan and Max Crumpton, which was a source of concern and disappointment for Baxter after the game.

However, he was keen to highlight the 'fantastic' performance of Woodburn, who provided the sort of display that he would reproduce throughout the season to see him go on and win the club's Player of the Year award, the recipient of which is chosen by the players themselves, and the Supporters' Club Player of the Year.

How he never got selected for England's end-of-season tour to Argentina, when many frontline players were missing on British and Irish Lions duty, will remain a mystery that only Eddie Jones has the answer to.

> You can coach a player as much as you like, but nine times out of ten, what a player achieves is down to their individual drive

It was not just his try-scoring ability that caught the eye, but also his security under the high ball.

"Olly is the classic example of why it is nice to be a coach," said Baxter. "I remember saying this in our very first season in the Premiership, after we had come out of the Championship, if you get game time in big Premiership and European games against good players, and with good players around you, it is a rare player that goes backwards under those circumstances.

"We found that, coming up from the Championship, what was important was to trust guys to go out there and play numerous minutes, and actually almost create Premiership players by the time they spent on the field, and I think Olly is the perfect example of that.

"What has hindered him more than anything else in his career is a lack of time on the field, and without that, you can't really closely analyse someone's game and challenge them over things they can improve.

"Ali Hepher is a top-quality backs coach, and when we were looking at Olly before he came to us, we obviously saw the good things in his game, but the truth of the matter was, we didn't see enough of them.

"I remember Ali sitting down with him in one of the very first meetings with him and saying: 'The big challenge for you if you want to be a regular starter is that we need more out of you. We see some good things in you, but we want more'.

"The most fantastic thing with Olly is how much he has added to his game over the time he has been with us, and hopefully will continue to add.

"He isn't someone who just stands on his wing and runs up and down the 15-metre channel. He wins back kick-offs for us, he makes covering tackles.

"In that Bristol game, he appeared on an inside shoulder and made a break to score a try, and those things are coming more and more into his game, and he is starting to show them on a regular basis.

"If you watch him carrying into contact now, compared to when he first came to us, he is aiming to get through multiple tackles, and realising it is not okay to just run forward and set the ball up and for us to keep possession, and those are all things you can challenge a player with when he is playing regularly.

"The player has obviously got to respond to that, and that is what he has done, He has come to us, he has done exactly what we have asked him to do, which is work extremely hard, he is a bigger physical specimen so he has worked hard in the gym, he has worked hard at conditioning, he has worked hard with the medical staff, and he has tidied up any little niggles he has had.

"Ali has worked very closely with him and keeps pushing him and he has shown fantastic individual drive to achieve bigger and better things.

"You can coach a player as much as you like, but nine times out of ten, what a player achieves is down their individual drive.

"He is a perfect example from within a team that decided to do something about it during the season. He did that by putting in performances week in and week out that made him Players' Player of the Year, which is the best thing you can get.

"He was one of a large group of players who took the season by the scruff of the neck, and they all ended up with great seasons."

Two bonus-point wins under their belts and Exeter were suddenly up to fifth place in the table, now only seven points behind new leaders Wasps and in the Champions Cup qualification places, making you wonder what all the early-season fuss had been about.

The corner appeared to have been turned, but Baxter and his fellow coaches were not convinced, and they still had this nagging feeling that things were still not quite right in the camp.

"Even though we won with a bonus point against Harlequins, it didn't feel like a great performance from us, and it didn't feel like we were absolutely bang on, and we conceded a lot of points," conceded Baxter.

"I thought the Bristol performance was good from us the week after. We came out of the blocks and really went after it, but again, later in the game, our level of performance wasn't quite so good.

"In a way our battle was that it was 'kind of okay', and that is sometimes the hardest thing to deal with, because you are always in this battle as a coach of not over-reacting but not under-reacting.

"Everything that was happening was saying to me 'if you go after the boys too much, it is going to be an over-reaction, but we need to do something because it doesn't feel quite right, and we must be careful we don't under-react'.

"That's where we were. We were in a bit of a no-man's-land really. Everything was okay. There wasn't anything to pull out.

"You couldn't say 'oh, our discipline is awful, or the guys are turning up late, or the guys don't care, or we have got loads of injuries'. There was no one thing you could put your finger on.

"I think this was where, as a coaching group, we started to know things weren't quite right, and I think the next couple of games really reinforced that."

A 20-19 defeat at Northampton, courtesy of a Harry Mallinder penalty two minutes from time, was followed by a 27-27 home draw against Gloucester.

The Cherry and Whites had led 27-14 at one stage in the second half, and Exeter were only saved by a try from Damian Welch 40 seconds from full time, with Steenson on this occasion missing the tricky touchline conversion that could have snatched an undeserved victory.

"I didn't think Northampton were playing that well, and we kind of found a way to lose that game, and then we were really challenged by Gloucester at home a week later and it ended up being a draw," said Baxter.

The Friday night match at Franklin's Gardens against the Saints was another strange affair in this early part of Exeter's season.

At times in the first half, the Chiefs played some superb rugby and they were well worthy of their 13-0 lead.

Saints had been forced into a very late change, with fly-half Stephen Myler dropping out, so England U20 captain Mallinder moved to the number 10 shirt and 20-year-old Rory Hutchinson came in for his Saints' league debut at inside centre, and they had no answer to Exeter in the early stages.

Two Steenson penalties and Woodburn's third try in two games, from Slade's fizzing, flat pass, had Exeter firmly in the driving seat after only 16 minutes.

But they allowed a Saints team, who were feeling the pressure from their own supporters after only winning one of their opening four league games, and that was at Bristol, to get back into the contest as they scored two converted tries in the space of only two minutes.

Wales and British and Irish Lions winger George North powered his way over in the left-hand corner for the first, and then straight from the restart, he set up the second with a devastating 55-metre break from inside his own 22, eluding two tackles, rounding Exeter full-back Turner and passing to South African scrum-half Nic Groom, who offloaded to Hutchinson, who raced over beside the posts for a stunning touchdown.

Mallinder converted both in Myler-esque fashion, and Saints suddenly had a 14-13 lead out of nowhere.

The second half was a real war of attrition, with two Steenson penalties to one by Mallinder edging Exeter back in front at 19-17.

The second of those for Steenson took him past an incredible landmark of 2,000 league and cup points for the Chiefs, but he was sadly to end up on the losing side.

Exeter centre Ollie Devoto was adjudged to have not rolled away from a tackle by referee Matt Carley, and with time fast running out, Mallinder made sure his dad, director of rugby Jim, got a much better night's sleep than he might have had otherwise by slotting the penalty to snatch victory.

Gloucester arrived at Sandy Park boasting a good record at the venue, and with the exception of Saracens, twice, they had been the only team to win there since January 2015.

Exeter received a blow before the game, with winger Nowell, having only returned from his broken thumb injury off the bench against Northampton for his first action of the season, suddenly sidelined again with a torn quad muscle after a brutal and controversial three-day England training camp in Brighton that also claimed Bath winger Anthony Watson (broken jaw) and Wasps flanker Sam Jones (fracturing his leg in a judo session) as victims.

A visibly annoyed Baxter, speaking straight after the Gloucester game, said: "He did it in training with England last Monday, and he was probably loaded in a way we wouldn't have loaded him, especially when he had only played his first bit of rugby back from injury last weekend against Northampton.

"More disappointingly, he was sent back to us with a report that they couldn't find any significant damage, and it was just a bit of loading and he was a bit sore.

"We fortunately scanned the injury and found a nine to 10-centimetre tear in his quad, so that is a significant injury and he is going to be out for a number of weeks."

For the second game running, Exeter came up against a side forced to make a very late change at fly-half, with Mark Atkinson promoted from the bench to wear the No.10 shirt in place of Billy Burns.

The first half was nip and tuck, with the visitors holding a 17-14 lead after tries by Scotland centre Matt Scott and winger Charlie Sharples, on his 200th appearance for the club, with Waldrom and Ian Whitten dotting down for the Chiefs.

Sharples' score was maybe fortuitous after the officials failed to spot a possible foot in touch by James Hook in the lead-up to the try.

But Gloucester pulled well clear after the break as the Chiefs contributed to their own downfall, giving Greig Laidlaw a very kickable penalty, and when Cowan-Dickie was uncharacteristically stripped of the ball by England No.8 Ben Morgan, who exchanged

Thomas Waldrom scoring against Gloucester on his 50th Premiership appearance for Chiefs

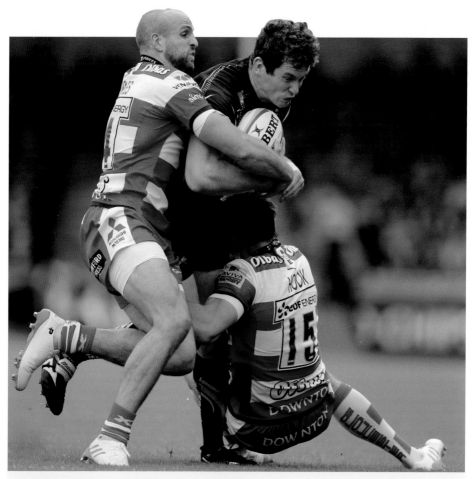

Ian Whitten had a big game against Gloucester, scoring two tries

passes down the touchline with Tongan winger David Halaifonua before scoring himself, and Laidlaw kicked the conversion, Gloucester had established a 27-14 advantage.

The Chiefs threw on some fresh legs, and the impact from the bench, together with some great character, saw them claw their way back into it.

A moment of magic 10 minutes from time by former Australian international Turner set up Whitten for his second try of the game, but when Steenson missed the touchline conversion and Exeter remained two scores behind, a losing bonus point looked to be the best they could achieve.

However, Steenson kept their hopes alive with a penalty seven minutes from time, and when they were awarded another on halfway with just over a minute to go, the Irishman smashed a massive touchfinder to five metres from the Gloucester line.

The Chiefs won the line-out, Welch (famously referred to by *BT Sport* commentator Nick Mullins in the past as 'running like a giraffe on steroids') was driven over, but Steenson's conversion from out wide was only just off target, leaving a share of the spoils between the two great West Country rivals.

That completed the first block of Premiership fixtures, and with only two victories and a draw from those games, Exeter found themselves down in fifth, four points outside the play-off places.

We are talking small margins, as turn those narrow defeats to Wasps and Northampton into wins, as well as the draw with Gloucester, and the extra eight points that would have gleaned would have placed Exeter second in the table.

But that nagging feeling Baxter had been experiencing since the final pre-season friendly at Rodney Parade that something was not quite right with his team was about to be acted upon, and with quite spectacular and unexpected results.

ROUND 1 – WASPS 25 EXETER CHIEFS 20
(Sunday, September 4, Ricoh Arena)

Wasps: R Miller; C Wade, E Daly, J Gopperth, J Bassett (F Halai 72); D Cipriani, D Robson (J Simpson 63); M Mullan (S McIntyre 53), T Taylor, P Swainston (M Moore 62); J Launchbury (capt), J Gaskell (M Symons 53); S Jones (A Rieder 75), G Thompson, N Hughes (A Johnson 62). Replacement (not used): B Macken.

Chiefs: P Dollman; O Woodburn, O Devoto, S Hill (G Steenson 74), I Whitten (J Short 11); H Slade, W Chudley (D Lewis 57); B Moon (A Hepburn 55), L Cowan-Dickie (J Yeandle 55), H Williams (G Holmes 52); M Lees (G Parling 47), D Welch; D Armand (capt), J Salvi, T Waldrom (D Dennis 64).

Wasps: Tries – Gopperth, Robson, Taylor; Conversions – Gopperth (2); Penalties – Gopperth (2).
Chiefs: Tries – Waldrom, Chudley; Conversions – Slade (2); Penalties – Slade (2).

HT: 8-17. **Referee:** Tom Foley (RFU). **Attendance:** 13,555.

ROUND 2 – EXETER CHIEFS 13 SARACENS 34
(Sunday, September 11, Sandy Park)

Chiefs: P Dollman (M Bodilly 15); L Turner, O Devoto, S Hill (G Steenson 61), I Whitten; H Slade, W Chudley (D Lewis 61); B Moon (A Hepburn 52), L Cowan-Dickie (J Yeandle 70), G Holmes (H Williams 50); G Parling (capt), D Welch   (M Lees 23-29, 50); D Armand (D Dennis 4-12), J Salvi (D Dennis 56), T Waldrom.

Saracens: A Goode; C Ashton, M Bosch (N Tompkins 78), B Barritt (capt, N Tompkins 4-12), S Maitland; A Lozowski (M Ellery 67), R Wigglesworth (B Spencer 63); M Vunipola (R Barrington 67), J George (S Brits 51), P Du Plessis (J Figallo ht); M Itoje, J Hamilton (M Rhodes 54); J Wray, S Burger (K Brown 67), B Vunipola.

Chiefs: Try – Cowan-Dickie; Conversion – Steenson; Penalties – Slade (2).
Saracens: Tries – Lozowski, Maitland (2), Wray, Spencer; Conversions – Goode (3); Penalty – Goode.

Yellow Card: Saracens – Wigglesworth.

HT: 6-12. **Referee:** JP Doyle (RFU). **Attendance:** 10,322.

ROUND 3 – EXETER CHIEFS 36 HARLEQUINS 25

(Saturday, September 17, Sandy Park)

Chiefs: L Turner (J Short 76); O Woodburn, O Devoto (S Hill 55), H Slade, I Whitten; G Steenson (capt), W Chudley (D Lewis 63); B Moon (A Hepburn 53), L Cowan-Dickie (J Yeandle 53), G Holmes (T Francis 53); G Parling, D Welch (O Atkins 66); D Armand (D Dennis 45), J Salvi (G Holmes 77), T Waldrom.

Harlequins: M Brown; M Yarde, J Marchant (Alofa Alofa 58), W Stanley (J Lang 76), C Walker; T Swiel, D Care (capt); J Marler (M Lambert 55), R Buchanan (D Ward 48), K Sinckler (W Collier 48); S Twomey (G Merrick 48), J Horwill; C Robshaw, L Wallace, J Clifford (J Chisholm 55). Replacement (not used): K Dickson.

Chiefs: Tries – Turner (2), Cowan-Dickie (3); Conversions – Steenson (4); Penalty – Steenson.
Harlequins: Tries – Buchanan, Care, Walker; Conversions – Swiel (2); Penalties – Swiel (2).

Red Card: Exeter – Francis.

HT: 29-13. **Referee:** Matt Carley (RFU). **Attendance:** 9,391.

ROUND 4 – BRISTOL 17 EXETER CHIEFS 41

(Friday, September 23, Ashton Gate)

Bristol: J Williams; R Edwards, W Hurrell, T Palamo, T Varndell (C Amesbury 2-12, 49); T Pisi, W Cliff (M Roberts 65, A Jarvis 80); K Traynor (S Tonga'uiha 60), R McMillan (M Crumpton 60), G Cortes (J Ford-Robinson 60); J Phillips, M Sorensen; J Fisher (J Joyce 65), J Lam (capt), J Crane (M Eadie 49).

Chiefs: L Turner (O Devoto 66); O Woodburn, S Hill (O Devoto 58-66), H Slade (J Short 68), I Whitten; G Steenson (capt), W Chudley (D Lewis 74); A Hepburn (B Moon 54), L Cowan-Dickie (J Yeandle 54), G Holmes (H Williams 54); M Lees, D Welch (G Parling 61); D Dennis, J Salvi (K Horstmann 67), T Waldrom.

Bristol: Tries – Williams, McMillan, Crumpton; Conversion – Williams.
Chiefs: Tries – Woodburn (2), Waldrom (2), Hill; Conversions – Steenson (5); Penalties – Steenson (2).

Yellow Card: Chiefs – Whitten 13.

HT: 5-24. **Referee:** Tom Foley (RFU). **Attendance:** 15,065.

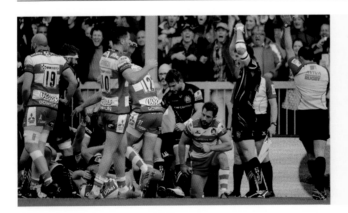

Exeter players celebrate Damian Welch's last-gasp try against Gloucester that earned them a draw

ROUND 5 –

NORTHAMPTON SAINTS 20 EXETER CHIEFS 19

(Friday, September 30, Franklin's Gardens)

Northampton: B Foden (capt, S Olver 69); K Pisi, G Pisi (A Tuala 62), R Hutchinson, G North; H Mallinder, N Groom (T Kessell 63); A Waller (C Ma'afu 27-33, 63), M Haywood, K Brookes (P Hill 58); C Lawes, M Paterson (S Dickenson 70); J Gibson, C Clark (T Harrison 59), L Picamoles. Replacement (not used): C Clare.

Chiefs: L Turner; O Woodburn, O Devoto (S Hill 24-31), H Slade, I Whitten (J Nowell 57); G Steenson (capt), W Chudley (D Lewis 20-27); B Moon (A Hepburn 48), J Yeandle (L Cowan-Dickie 48), G Holmes (H Williams 60); M Lees (D Welch 59), G Parling; D Dennis, K Horstmann, T Waldrom (B White 78).

Northampton: Tries – North, Hutchinson; Conversions – Mallinder (2); Penalties – Mallinder (2). **Chiefs:** Try – Woodburn; Conversion – Steenson; Penalties – Steenson (4).

HT: 14-13. **Referee:** Matt Carley (RFU). **Attendance:** 13,901.

ROUND 6 – EXETER CHIEFS 27 GLOUCESTER 27

(Saturday, October 8, Sandy Park)

Chiefs: L Turner; O Woodburn, S Hill, H Slade (O Devoto 59), I Whitten; G Steenson (capt), W Chudley (D Lewis 59), B Moon (C Rimmer 70), L Cowan-Dickie (J Yeandle 66), G Holmes (H Williams 59); M Lees (D Welch 51), G Parling; D Dennis (K Horstmann 20-27, 51), J Salvi, T Waldrom. Replacement (not used): M Bodilly.

Gloucester: J Hook; C Sharples (O Thorley 71), M Scott, B Twelvetrees, D Halaifonua; M Atkins, G Laidlaw (capt); P McAllister (Y Thomas 49), R Hibbard (M Matu'u 42-48, 67), P Doran-Jones; T Savage (J Latta 57), M Galarza; R Moriarty, J Rowan (M Kvesic 60), B Morgan. Replacements (not used): N Thomas, W Heinz, L Ludlow.

Chiefs: Tries – Waldrom, Whitten (2), Welch; Conversions – Steenson (2); Penalty – Steenson. **Gloucester:** Tries – Scott, Sharples, Morgan; Conversions – Laidlaw (3); Penalties – Twelvetrees, Laidlaw.

HT: 14-17. **Referee:** Greg Garner (RFU). **Attendance:** 11,934.

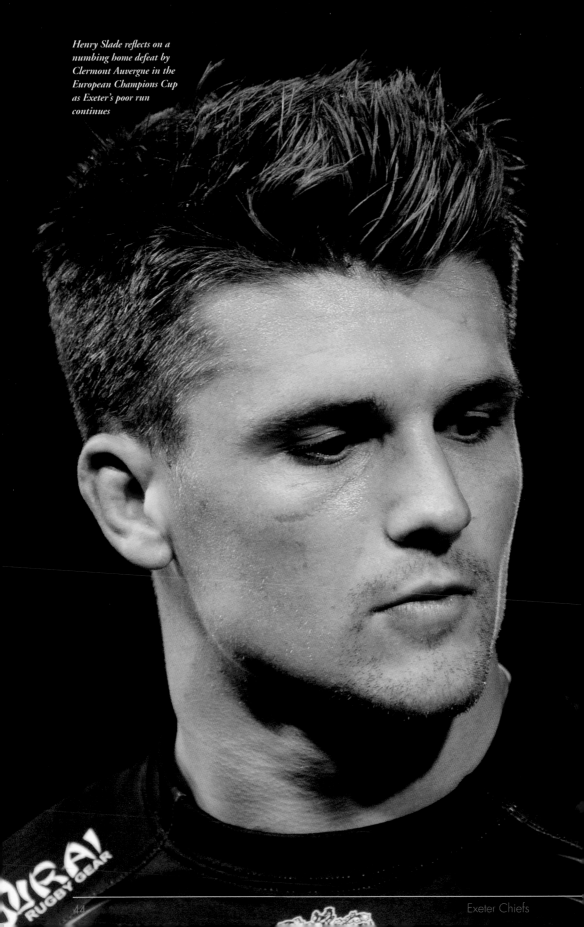

Henry Slade reflects on a numbing home defeat by Clermont Auvergne in the European Champions Cup as Exeter's poor run continues

CHAPTER 4

Watershed Moment

PREMIERSHIP TABLE							
	P	**W**	**D**	**L**	**F**	**A**	**Pts**
Saracens	7	6	0	1	199	69	29
Wasps	7	6	0	1	241	133	28
Bath	7	6	0	1	185	94	26
Leicester	7	4	0	3	182	163	19
Sale	7	3	1	3	151	162	18
Harlequins	7	4	0	3	147	154	17
EXETER	**7**	**2**	**1**	**4**	**166**	**161**	**16**
Northampton	7	3	0	4	125	134	15
Newcastle	7	3	0	4	89	158	14
Gloucester	7	1	2	4	146	157	12
Worcester	7	1	2	4	120	208	9
Bristol	7	0	0	7	95	253	2

OCTOBER

Sunday 16	ECC	L	Exeter Chiefs 8	Clermont Auvergne 35
Saturday 22	ECC	L	Ulster 19	Exeter Chiefs 18
Sunday 30	AP	L	Exeter Chiefs 10	Bath 13

NOVEMBER

Saturday 5	AWC	L	Harlequins 29	Exeter Chiefs 15
Sunday 13	AWC	W	Exeter Chiefs 62	Cardiff Blues 25

Premiership points available 5 – points taken 1

IT has been well documented that what happened next was a crucial moment in Exeter's season.

It was not so much the size of the 35-8 European Champions Cup defeat to Clermont Auvergne that was worrying.

After all, they were one of the best sides in European rugby, and proved that again by going on to reach the final at Murrayfield, where they lost to Saracens.

By the end of the season, they had beaten Exeter five times on the six occasions the two sides had met in the group stages of the Champions Cup/Heineken Cup over a five-year period, with the Chiefs' only success a 31-14 triumph in December 2015.

When I commentated on them, I was almost drooling in anticipation as the names of the likes of Fofana, Parra, Rougerie, Abendanon, Lopez, Kayser, Chouly and Nakaitaci slipped off my tongue.

The list was endless, such was the quality they had at their disposal, so it was no disgrace losing to them, by whatever margin.

It was the level of performance, though, that was most disturbing.

Exeter had their injuries going into the game, and suffered another blow when Luke Cowan-Dickie hobbled off after half an hour with a twisted ankle, so it was always going to be a tall order to beat the Frenchmen.

But it was a very un-Exeter-like display and you could sense from the crowd that people were starting to get very worried at the Chiefs' lack of form.

Baxter also expressed his own concern straight after a game in which the Chiefs had conceded five converted tries.

"I don't think that was anything like the level of performance we can achieve or have achieved in the past," he said.

"We huffed and puffed at times, but there were a lot of errors in there, and our Achilles heel this season of conceding soft points out of innocuous situations reared its ugly head again.

"We are still probably a team dealing with having a really good season for the first time, and we are not dealing with it as well as we could, and with some fight and anger."

It was in the light of the Clermont game that Baxter finally decided it was time to do something about this uneasy feeling that he had been experiencing for several weeks.

However, he admitted there had already been plenty going on behind the scenes in the lead-up to that European fixture as the coaching staff grappled with the issue of what exactly was the matter with their off-colour team.

"It was after we were well beaten by Clermont that we decided to sit down and make a bit of a change, but I think a lot of the important chats happened a little bit before then," recalled Baxter.

"I remember sitting in a coaching meeting and saying that results weren't going the way we wanted them to, and having finished second in the league the season before, to suddenly be bumbling around in the bottom half of the table, even though it was only a few games into the season, didn't feel right, and it didn't feel like we were getting the results we had the season before, and everyone started getting a bit defensive.

"Ali (Hepher) said we didn't want to start tinkering too much, because if we did we were just creating more doubt and uncertainty.

"I had a chat with Rob (Hunter) about our set piece, and said to him: 'It doesn't feel like we are trying to be the most dominant set piece we can be'.

"I said to them: 'Let's not hide behind stats. Let's talk about how it feels. Does it feel like we have got a dominant scrum, a dominant line-out, a dominant pack of forwards? Does it feel like our attack is fluent?'

"We had a little moment where everyone was a bit edgy and a bit defensive, but we came through it.

"It is great credit to Rob and Ali that they sat there and said: 'It does actually need to be a bit more about how it feels, and it doesn't just have to be stats-based, where the line-out stats are saying we are still producing good ball, the scrum stats are saying we are still doing okay, and the attack stats say we are still scoring so many tries.

"It showed the strength of us as a coaching group, and Ricky (Pellow) as well, that we could sit there and have what wasn't a ridiculously heated dispute but it was a little bit fraught and a little bit testy, and come through it.

"I remember saying: 'Are we all going to be so defensive on our own bits of the game that we are responsible for that we actually can't talk to each other or put an idea out there?'

"I think everyone stopped at that moment, drew breath, and agreed 'there are some things we can do as a coaching group to change things'.

"I said: 'Let's start talking about how we feel we are playing, not just what the stats say. At the same time, I will start to do a bit of work on what was our issue, what hadn't we dealt with, what hadn't we looked at?'.

"I started looking for things on the internet about how do you approach losing a final in terms of how it drives you the following season? How can you use the hurt from the year before as a positive? Have we approached things the right way as a coaching team?'"

Throughout his coaching career, Baxter has never been afraid to use modern technology to help put a point across to his players or inspire them with a piece of video footage.

At a dinner at Sandy Park during the season, he gave a fascinating talk on how the club had progressed from a Championship side to being beaten Premiership finalists, and showed several musical montages of the best bits of various matches and seasons throughout the years.

"When you are sat in a meeting with players, you can say 'this is what I think has happened', or you can show them something that triggers things, and I was looking for clips on the internet to help me with that," he said.

However, the piece of footage he found to help inspire his players came from a very unlikely source, and a totally different sport – American football.

An Emmy Award-winning series on US television, called 'America's Game', delves deep into the story behind the making of Super Bowl champions. Each episode is a 60-minute documentary featuring key members of the winning team telling behind-the-scenes accounts from their championship season.

One that particularly caught Baxter's eye was Seattle Seahawks' first, and at the time of writing, only Super Bowl success, in the 2013-14 NFL season.

Their triumph had its foundations in a play-off match against Atlanta Falcons the previous season, where they were down by 20 points in the fourth quarter, but they came back to register one of the greatest comebacks in play-off history.

However, their remarkable display of fight and courage ended in heartbreak, as a defensive breakdown late in the game saw them suffer a 30-28 defeat.

The following season they tied with the Denver Broncos for a NFL-best regular season record of 13 wins and three defeats, won both of their play-off games, and crushed Denver 43-8 in the final to win their first Super Bowl Championship in one of the most one-sided contests in the competition's history (they also reached the Super Bowl the year after, but this time they went down 28-24 to New England Patriots).

"I watched that footage and thought 'wow, what a parallel that is to what happened to us in the Twickenham final against Saracens'," said Baxter.

"With Seattle it wasn't a final, it was a knockout match on the way to the Super Bowl, but it was like us against Saracens, where we got blown away a little bit, made a comeback and got to within one score of winning it, and then the heartbreak at the end where the chance of victory was taken away from us by Saracens' late try.

"It was the response of Seattle to that setback, though, that I wanted our players to see."

The clip that Baxter played to his squad in the aftermath of the Clermont game was an interview with Seattle cornerback Richard Sherman.

"Myself and Earl Thomas sat in the locker room for about three hours after that Atlanta game, and just said: 'We will never lose again in the play-offs. We will punish whoever gets in our way. We know we are a better team than that'," revealed Sherman.

Baxter added: "In our first meeting with the players after Clermont, I said to the lads that I was quite prepared to take a lot of the responsibility for what had happened, because I had never sussed it out and I had never felt that was the response that there needed to be after losing the final, but I said: 'How many of you sat in that Twickenham changing room and looked at each other and said: "I never want to feel this way again and I am going to do something about it?" For how many of you has that been your reaction? Or how many of you have said to yourselves "I have had a good season", and drew a bit of breath?'

"I can still remember the look on the faces of so many of the guys in that team meeting, who had been with us for so long and achieved their best ever season and gone off and played international rugby.

"Richard Sherman was one of the leaders of the Seattle team, and he sat there for two or three hours and was almost inconsolable at losing the game, and those players made a vow to each other that they would not be in that situation again and lose.

"Now, you can't make it happen just by saying it, but as I looked around that team room – and we have got a good group of players, who are good men and are very honest – you could actually see them looking at each other and thinking 'this is exactly what I have done. I had a really good season last year, I have kind of trained okay this season, but I haven't really decided that this is what I am going to make it all about'.

"That was also the time when we decided to change what we were going to talk about as our driver, as our goal.

"The word 'trust' was a big driver for us – you show the qualities as a player and as a man that other people can trust you. Trust is a feeling, and you will only trust me if I show you I am trustworthy. I can't tell you to trust me, because that creates doubt more than anything else, but I can show you by how I train and how I play.

"Trust is still a driver for us in the background, but that day, on the Monday after the Clermont game (Monday, October 17, to be exact), I told the players that we are now only going to talk about how we build champions.

"There is no point us talking about much else because we lost the final.

"We can talk about all the qualities we want to have as a group, but the reality is they should all be leading to one thing, and that is 'what are we going to do to become champions?'

"I make a musical montage for every game we win, and along the bottom of the screen for each match after the meeting it said: 'Building Champions'."

The psychology involved in sport these days is incredible, and the ways to keep that goal firmly fixed in the minds of the players did not stop there.

"One of the things we did to remind the players of this every day is in the players' corridor underneath the main stand," explained Baxter.

"On the right-hand side as you walk towards the changing room is a picture of all of the Chiefs' teams year by year. The history of where we have been as a club and all the things we have achieved, is very important to me, and very important to us as a club.

"But, as you walk into the home changing room, there is a blank picture frame on the wall, and I said to the guys when I put it up that it would only be filled by a team that wins the Premiership. That is going to be a symbol when you come in here every day because you are going to ask yourselves why there is a blank frame?

"We just said and did a few things like that, and we were prepared to sit there and talk about all the qualities we needed to show to be champions, and we were not going to be driven by anything else.

"It was a seminal moment, but it meant something because the players were prepared to buy into it very, very quickly."

However, even though everyone acknowledges the Clermont game as a watershed moment that led to the Chiefs eventually winning the Premiership crown, Baxter said that was only a part of the story.

A revitalised group of players, fired up by their newly-defined goal, went on to lose their next two games.

They travelled to Belfast the following weekend and suffered an agonising 19-18 defeat away to Ulster in the Champions Cup, courtesy of a Paddy Jackson drop goal a minute from time, which robbed Exeter fly-half Gareth Steenson of a happy homecoming to his native Northern Ireland.

It was an emotional day as, just before kick-off, both clubs had marked the incredibly sad death the previous weekend of Ireland hero and Munster head coach Anthony Foley to a heart condition in a Paris hotel only hours before their Champions Cup game at Racing 92.

Steenson, playing against the club where he started his career as an Academy youngster, looked to have won the game in the 77th minute with his own drop goal, and even after Jackson's successful kick, Steenson thought he had found the target again with another drop-goal effort from 40 metres.

He started celebrating straight away as he struck the ball really well, but it drifted a whisker off target at the last moment, denying the Chiefs a famous win.

It was a sinking feeling that Exeter Chiefs communications manager Mark Stevens cleverly linked, in his match report on the club website, to the fact that the game was being played in the city where the ill-fated Titanic was built.

That was hard enough to take for Exeter, but what followed eight days later at Sandy Park was even more gut-wrenching as powerful Army and England winger Semesa Rokoduguni brushed aside a couple of poor tackles by Gareth Steenson and Olly Woodburn in the eighth minute of injury time to give Bath a 13-10 victory over their West Country rivals in the Premiership.

Exeter had lost experienced Australian flanker Julian Salvi in the Belfast battle to a torn bicep that was to rule him out until early February, but the Chiefs handed young scrum-half Jack Maunder – the son of former Exeter legend Andy – a Premiership debut off the bench, after giving him his first taste of first-team action against Clermont.

Exeter had looked on course for a deserved victory, with a Mitch Lees try and five points from the boot of Steenson, until Rokoduguni's late, late intervention.

It left them with only one win in five home games in all competitions in the 2016-17 season – hardly Fortress Sandy Park.

It was a defeat that also dropped them to seventh place in the table, well adrift of the top three, outside the play-off positions, and even a point adrift of the Champions Cup qualification spots.

"You could see how quickly the players were prepared to buy into what we were saying after that Clermont game when we went to Ulster the following week and, I am not saying we were perfect but, the spirit, the fight, the work rate and the guts and determination to try and drive a win there was fantastic," said Baxter.

"When you think we lost to a relatively late drop goal, and just by the width of a post missed the chance to win it, and how well Ulster beat Clermont there later on in the pool (39-32), you can see what a fantastic flip in mentality happened in that short period of time in that group of players.

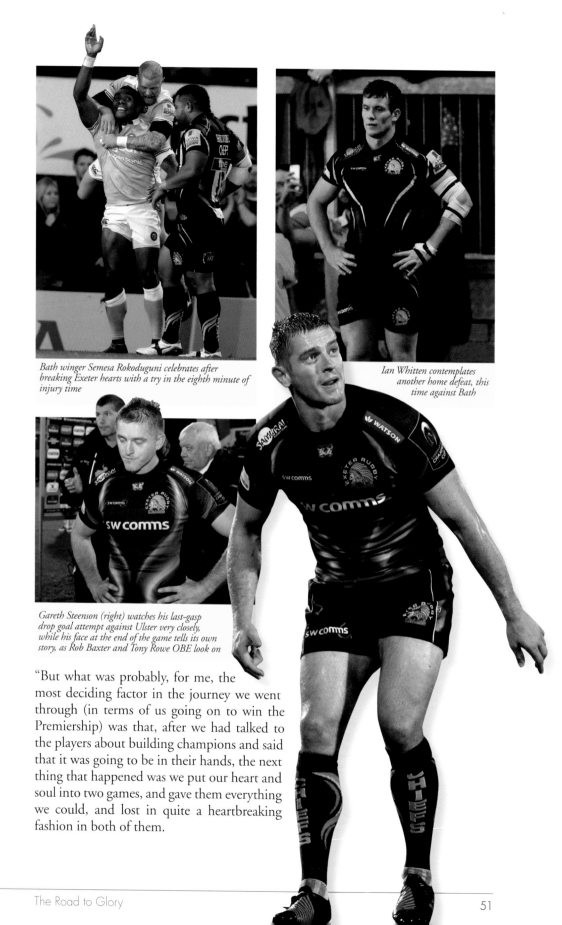

Bath winger Semesa Rokoduguni celebrates after breaking Exeter hearts with a try in the eighth minute of injury time

Ian Whitten contemplates another home defeat, this time against Bath

Gareth Steenson (right) watches his last-gasp drop goal attempt against Ulster very closely, while his face at the end of the game tells its own story, as Rob Baxter and Tony Rowe OBE look on

"But what was probably, for me, the most deciding factor in the journey we went through (in terms of us going on to win the Premiership) was that, after we had talked to the players about building champions and said that it was going to be in their hands, the next thing that happened was we put our heart and soul into two games, and gave them everything we could, and lost in quite a heartbreaking fashion in both of them.

"There were lads in tears after the Ulster away game because we had put so much into it emotionally.

"For them to be able to lose those two games but keep driving on like they did says more about us as a side than anything else, because after that Bath match we didn't lose another Premiership game, even though we were only a third of the way through the season at that stage.

"The players deserve so much credit for being able to talk so openly about what we felt were our issues, and to take that on board, and for it not to be immediately successful on the pitch, but to still drive forward.

"It was immediately successful, though, in terms of the level of our performances, and I thought our display against Ulster was a world apart from what it had been a few weeks before.

"Our performance against Bath as well, although we made some mistakes, it never really merited us losing the game.

"I actually quite enjoyed talking to the players after the Ulster and Bath games, because I remember saying after the Ulster match: 'You have given us something to work with now, with the effort and the emotion you have put into today, to move forward with'.

"It is not that the players weren't trying before, but in top-level sport you are talking about a one, two or three per cent difference in training and playing.

"We didn't suddenly change all 15 players and pick a different team. It was the same guys, but just a little bit more focused and a little bit more driven, and with a little bit of a different game plan.

"We talked about being a little bit more aggressive, about being the team going out to dominate games, and we talked a lot about each player's individual role in driving us forward and carrying us up the field in attack and defence.

"The technicalities of the game are a lot more complex, and you deal with those day by day, but we kept the emotional side of things very simple, in terms of driving us up the field, and the players really took that on board, and we kind of flourished from then on.

"And that, for me from a coaching perspective, is kind of very much the story of the season – what happened over that block of a few weeks because, from then on, we very much drove it, and we probably only had a couple of potential hiccup moments in the course of the rest of the season.

"I think the only wobbles we had were in the Champions Cup, and in and around our Anglo-Welsh Cup run, when we reached the semi-final and final and then had Sale and Bristol at home in the Premiership, and we probably did under-perform, but again, we took that head on."

I will return to that period around the Anglo-Welsh Cup final in the following chapters, as it also played a very important part in the final, wonderful outcome of the season.

Jonny Hill feels the full force of tackles from Harlequins duo Charlie Matthews (left) and James Chisholm

Jack Maunder shows his speed of pass against Harlequins on his first start for the Chiefs

Tom Lawday scores his first Chiefs' try in the match against Cardiff Blues

Before Exeter returned to Premiership action, they began their Anglo-Welsh Cup campaign – no longer LV= after the ending of the sponsorship deal with the insurance company – with their opening two pool matches.

They started with a televised Saturday evening trip to Harlequins, where they went down to a 29-15 defeat to make it six games in all competitions without a victory – a run unheard of since the Chiefs had been in the top flight.

James Short was the only survivor from the starting line-up that had faced Bath, and Chiefs were able to welcome back Phil Dollman and Dave Ewers from injury, the latter for his first appearance of the season, while Maunder and Shaun Malton made their first senior starts for the club.

There were also first-team debuts off the bench for Academy youngsters Joe Simmonds, Harry Strong and Tom Lawday.

Young Joe Simmonds marked his home debut with a man-of-the-match display against Cardiff Blues

However, the game will perhaps most be remembered for a dreadful high tackle by Quins' Kiwi No.8 Mat Luamanu on Exeter fly-half Will Hooley after only eight minutes that was to rule the Chiefs youngster out until January with concussion.

Amazingly, Welsh referee Craig Evans only brandished a yellow card after reviewing the incident on the big screen with the television match official, when many felt it was a clear red-card offence.

Luamanu was subsequently banned by the Rugby Football Union for five weeks after being found guilty of dangerous tackling, which just shows how badly wrong the officials got it on the night.

The RFU ruling was little consolation to Exeter as the result would no doubt have been very different at the Twickenham Stoop had they played for 72 minutes against only 14 men.

As it turned out, the loss to Harlequins was their only defeat in the competition until they reached the final, and they exacted some sweet revenge on Quins in the semi-final at Sandy Park.

What followed next was more like the Exeter Chiefs that the supporters had grown to love watching over the previous few years.

They took apart an admittedly very young and inexperienced Cardiff Blues – whose first-team squad were on holiday – 62-25 at Sandy Park, running in 10 tries, with six of them converted by young Joe Simmonds in a man-of-the-match display on his first start for the club.

In fact, it was a great day all around for Exeter's Academy, with Billy Keast another making his first start, while Will Norton, Josh Caulfield, Jack Innard, Marcus Street and Harvey Skinner all came off the bench for their first taste of senior action.

There was also a first-team debut for Exeter University tight-head prop Jack Owlett, while Lawday and Innard scored their first tries for the club.

In addition, there was a first outing of the season for Joe's older brother Sam Simmonds, who was to play such an important part in Exeter's run-in to Premiership glory.

Despite the emphatic scoreline, the Chiefs still managed to give their supporters a scare as they trailed 10-0 after only four minutes before clicking into gear.

The victory continued their astonishing run of success against Welsh clubs since coming up into the Premiership, with only one defeat in 14 matches against sides from the Principality – away to Ospreys in the 2015-16 European Champions Cup.

It was in between the two cup games that the Chiefs announced the signing of Fijian international scrum-half/winger Niko Matawalu from Premiership rivals Bath, in the hope that he would add an 'X factor' to their backline.

However, a broken hand suffered in an A League game and Exeter's great run of form until the end of the season, meant he was never seen in a first-team shirt before being released at the end of the campaign.

EUROPEAN CHAMPIONS CUP
ROUND 1 – EXETER CHIEFS 8 CLERMONT AUVERGNE 35
(Sunday, October 16, Sandy Park)

Chiefs: L Turner (M Bodilly 53); O Woodburn, O Devoto, S Hill, I Whitten; G Steenson (capt, H Slade 57), D Lewis (J Maunder 57); M Low (C Rimmer 53), L Cowan-Dickie (J Yeandle 30), H Williams (G Holmes 53); G Parling, D Welch (M Lees 57); K Horstmann, J Salvi, T Waldrom (D Dennis 57).

Clermont Auvergne: N Abendanon; D Strettle, R Lamerat (A Rougerie 61), W Fofana, N Nakaitaci; C Lopez (P Fernandez 65), M Parra (L Radosavljevic 67); T Domingo (E Falgoux 52), B Kayser (N Charles 69), D Zirakashvili (C Ric 61); F Van Der Merwe, S Vahaamahina; D Chouly (capt) (P Jedrasik 53), J Bardy, F Lee (A Lapandry 47).

Chiefs: Try – Hill; Penalty – Steenson.
Clermont: Tries – Bardy, Nakaitaci, Fofana (2), Abendanon; Conversions – Parra (4), Fernandez.

Yellow Card: Clermont – Van Der Merwe.

HT: 3-21. **Referee:** George Clancy (Ire). **Attendance:** 9,879.

The faces of Harry Williams (left) and Greg Holmes at the end of the Clermont game say it all. What's happening?

ROUND 2 – ULSTER 19 EXETER CHIEFS 18

(Saturday, October 22, Kingspan Stadium)

Ulster: J Payne; A Trimble (capt) (C Gilroy 68), L Marshall (T Bowe 79), S Olding, C Piutau; P Jackson, R Pienaar; K McCall, R Best (R Herring 67), R Ah You (R Kane ht-46, 49-52, A Warwick 79); P Browne (A O'Connor 13-20, 22), F Van der Merwe; I Henderson (C Ross ht), S Reidy, R Wilson. Replacement (not used): P Marshall.

Chiefs: L Turner; O Woodburn, I Whitten (O Devoto 64), H Slade, J Short; G Steenson (capt), D Lewis (J Maunder 64); M Low (C Rimmer 49), J Yeandle, H Williams (T Francis 49); M Lees (J Hill 64), G Parling; K Horstmann, J Salvi (D Dennis 51), T Waldrom. Replacements (not used): E Taione, S Hill.

Ulster: Try – Reidy; Conversion – Jackson; Penalties – Jackson (3); Drop-Goal – Jackson.
Chiefs: Penalties – Steenson (5); Drop Goal – Steenson.

HT: 10-6. **Referee:** Alexandre Ruiz (France). **Attendance:** 16,843.

PREMIERSHIP

ROUND 7 – EXETER CHIEFS 10 BATH 13

(Sunday, October 30, Sandy Park)

Chiefs: L Turner (O Devoto 28); O Woodburn, I Whitten, H Slade, J Short (S Hill 61), G Steenson (capt), D Lewis (J Maunder 47); M Low (C Rimmer 44), J Yeandle (E Taione 28-35, ht), H Williams (T Francis 47); M Lees, G Parling (J Hill 54); D Dennis (B White 76), K Horstmann, T Waldrom.

Bath: T Homer; S Rokoduguni, J Joseph, M Banahan, A Brew (J Williams 68); G Ford, K Fotuali'i; N Auterac (M Lahiff 58), R Batty (T Dunn 53), H Thomas (K Palma-Newport 38-40, 68); L Charteris (E Stooke 53), D Attwood; M Garvey (capt), T Ellis (G Mercer 76), C Ewels. Replacements (not used): W Homer, R Priestland.

Chiefs: Try – Lees; Conversion – Steenson; Penalty – Steenson.
Bath: Try – Rokoduguni; Conversion – Ford; Penalties – Ford (2).

HT: 3-0. **Referee:** Ian Tempest (RFU). **Attendance:** 12,284.

One positive from the Clermont hammering was a first-team debut for young Jack Maunder, seen here getting some advice from Gareth Steenson

ANGLO-WELSH CUP

ROUND 1 – HARLEQUINS 29 EXETER CHIEFS 15

(Saturday, November 5, Twickenham Stoop)

Harlequins: A Morris; C Walker, J Marchant (L Jones 43), J Lang, Alofa Alofa (R Chisholm 2, R Jackson ht); N Evans, C Mulchrone; M Lambert (O Evans 76), J Gray (C Piper 76), W Collier (A Jones 76); C Matthews, S South (M Reddish 37); J Chisholm (G Naoupu 76), D Ward (capt), M Luamanu.

Chiefs: P Dollman (H Strong 31); M Bodilly, O Devoto, S Hill (S Townsend 73), J Short; W Hooley (J Simmonds 8), J Maunder (capt); B Moon (B Keast 73), S Malton (E Taione 50), G Holmes (M Low 59); O Atkins (D Welch 54), J Hill; D Ewers (S Malton 65-72), B White (T Lawday 65), T Johnson.

Harlequins: Tries – Morris, Walker, L Jones; Conversion – Evans; Penalties – Evans (4).
Chiefs: Tries – Short, Taione; Conversion – J Simmonds; Penalty – J Simmonds.

Yellow Cards: Harlequins – Luamanu; Chiefs – Taione.

HT: 11-5. **Referee:** Craig Evans (Wales). **Attendance:** 8,000.

ROUND 2 – EXETER CHIEFS 62 CARDIFF BLUES 25

(Sunday, November 13, Sandy Park)

Chiefs: P Dollman (H Strong ht); M Bodilly, M Campagnaro (H Skinner 59), T Hendrickson, I Whitten (T Lawday 67); J Simmonds, W Chudley (S Townsend ht); B Keast (W Norton 72), S Malton (J Innard 59), J Owlett (M Street 72); O Atkins (J Caulfield 59), D Welch; B White, S Simmonds, T Johnson (capt).

Cardiff Blues: R Williams; A Summerhill (O Lane 33), H Millard, G Smith (capt), J Beal; J Evans (B Jones 11), D Blacker (R Davies 67); B Thyer (R Carre 63), K Myhill (L Belcher 62), D Lewis (A Peikrishvili 53); J Davies, J Down; S Davies, Lewis-Hughes, J Sheekey (L Belcher 16-25, H Barnes 55). Replacement (not used): M Sieniawski.

Chiefs: Tries – Malton, penalty try, Campagnaro, Welch, S Simmonds, Hendrickson, Townsend, Johnson, Innard, Lawday; Conversions – J Simmonds (6).
Cardiff: Tries – Sheekey, Beal, Williams (2); Conversion – Evans; Penalty – Evans.

Yellow Cards: Cardiff - Myhill, R Davies.

HT: 31-10. **Referee:** Luke Pearce (RFU). **Attendance:** 9,595.

Is it Alan Shearer?!
Thomas Waldrom triggers
memories of the former
England striker with his
try celebration against
the Warriors

CHAPTER 5

Normal Service Resumed

PREMIERSHIP TABLE							
	P	W	D	L	F	A	Pts
Saracens	10	8	0	2	262	116	38
Wasps	10	8	0	2	319	205	37
Bath	10	8	0	2	235	135	35
Leicester	10	7	0	3	247	196	31
EXETER	**10**	**5**	**1**	**4**	**276**	**205**	**30**
Harlequins	10	5	0	5	206	237	23
Newcastle	10	5	0	5	168	238	23
Gloucester	10	3	2	5	228	217	23
Northampton	10	4	0	6	170	192	20
Sale	10	3	1	6	191	245	18
Worcester	10	1	2	7	171	309	10
Bristol	10	0	0	10	138	316	4

NOVEMBER

Friday 18	AP	W	Newcastle Falcons 19	Exeter Chiefs 32
Saturday 26	AP	W	Exeter Chiefs 57	Worcester Warriors 22

DECEMBER

Friday 2	AP	W	Sale Sharks 3	Exeter Chiefs 21
Sunday 11	ECC	L	Exeter Chiefs 7	Bordeaux-Begles 13
Saturday 17	ECC	W	Bordeaux-Begles 12	Exeter Chiefs 20

Premiership points available 15 – points taken 14

THE Anglo-Welsh Cup try feast against Cardiff Blues meant Exeter Chiefs went into their next block of Premiership fixtures in buoyant mood.

Trips to Newcastle Falcons and Sale Sharks, with a visit from Worcester Warriors sandwiched in between, were three games that any side looking to lift the Premiership trophy should really be winning.

But Sale were two points and two places ahead of the Chiefs in the table after seven rounds of the season, while a revitalised Newcastle, playing some of their best rugby for years, knew a victory over Exeter would see them leapfrog the Chiefs in the standings.

Exeter were on fire at a bitterly cold Kingston Park, with Thomas Waldrom credited with this touchdown against Newcastle from a driving maul

Rob Baxter was well aware of the Chiefs' standing in the table at that stage, and how crucial the Newcastle game was.

"I remember saying to Rob Hunter (Northumbrian born and bred) during the week leading up to the Newcastle game, if we don't knock in some points on Friday night and other teams below us do, the way the fixtures have fallen, we could end up 10th in the table after this weekend and right down in the relegation battle," recalled Baxter.

"It was not until after the game, which we won, he said to me: 'You had me a bit worried there, as though you were saying I wonder what the reaction of everyone will be if we don't win this game?'

"I was kind of just saying it in conversation, and there wasn't genuinely any more to it than that, other than 'this will be an interesting scenario for us to fight our way out of if we don't come through this'."

Exeter had also had trouble in previous seasons capturing victories at places where they had been expected to win, like London Irish in the 2014-15 campaign.

They had only lost one of their 10 previous Premiership meetings with the Falcons, and that was at Kingston Park in October 2014, but Newcastle had beaten Sale at home, only lost by a point to Leicester, and won at Gloucester in the opening weeks of the season.

"By the time we went to Newcastle, we as a first team had locked down that the season was ours, for what we wanted to make of it," explained Baxter.

"The Anglo-Welsh Cup fixtures allowed our frontline group of players to spend a genuine bit of time training together and put themselves in that scenario where they were saying: 'We kind of get where we are going now. We are putting the emotional side of things right back at the forefront and we know where we want to be.'

Newcastle's Sinoti Sinoti is left for dead by another spectacular James Short try

"We had a period of time leading into that Newcastle game where the frontline players had had a bit of a rest-up and some tough stuff in training as well.

"The Newcastle game was really good for us in a way because everyone was talking about how good Newcastle were playing, so that created a really good challenge for us.

"Newcastle built it up to be a really big game (they billed it as 'The Big Night Out', staging a university match on the Kingston Park pitch prior to kick-off to encourage the fans to get to the stadium early and create an intimidating atmosphere), with their biggest crowd of the season, but that really suited us.

"We talked that match up as a being a big game for a long time, and we went there and played really well in the circumstances, and that really showed that we had made the season about us.

"All we talked about in the build-up to that game was 'our forwards are going to take them on; if we get opportunities we are going to kick to the corner; we are going to go for drives; we are going to try and push them around in the scrum and win penalties from it, which will give us territory; we are going to be positive in everything we do playing wise'.

"I think, by then, things had started to align for us. As individuals, the players were saying: 'It is me who has got to carry us forward, and not the guy next to me or someone else. If I get into a scrum or maul, it is my job to drive the opposition back or drive us forward'.

"We had simplified things, and people were just very driven and focused on their individual performances."

Baxter had asked his players in the media before the game to "start accelerating through the Premiership season".

Ollie Devoto leaves Newcastle's Marcus Watson and Mike Delany in his wake as he races 70 metres to score an interception try

The team had flown up the day before the contest, and he wanted his players to get off to a flying start in the match, as they had done just over 12 months before at the same venue, when they had the four-try bonus point all wrapped up inside the opening 30 minutes on their way to a 41-3 success.

It was another nightmare Friday night journey up the UK's overcrowded motorway system for the supporters' coach – and every single one of those fans deserved a medal for embarking on Exeter's longest Premiership trip of the season.

They had perhaps cut it a bit fine by not leaving Apple Lane in Exeter until 10am, but even so, they would have expected to have got to the ground in time for the 8pm kick-off.

As it was, the Chiefs got off to such a fantastic start that many of those fans watched their heroes' opening try of the game, a somewhat fortuitous 70-metre interception score by Ollie Devoto after only three minutes, as they got off the coach in the Newcastle club car park, as it was played out on the big screen at one end of the ground!

In fact, my regular *BBC Radio Devon* summariser, John Lockyer, had not even spotted that, and in fact thought Newcastle had scored the first try until I put him right when he joined me at the commentary position!

The game also showed what tremendous depth the Chiefs had in their squad, as Jack Nowell, Henry Slade, Dave Ewers, Don Armand, Julian Salvi, Sam Hill, Luke Cowan-Dickie, Tomas Francis, Elvis Taione and Moray Low were all missing through either injury or autumn international call-ups.

The final winning margin could have been even more against a surprisingly poor Newcastle side, as three times Exeter kicked penalties to the corner, only to make a mess of the five-metre line-out.

Devoto's score – his first in Exeter colours since his summer move from Bath – and a fifth league try of the season for Thomas Waldrom, from Exeter's driving maul, plus two Gareth Steenson conversions, helped Exeter into a 14-8 interval lead on a bitterly cold night on Tyneside, with Scott Lawson dotting down for the hosts.

Two penalties from Steenson's boot saw the Chiefs move 20-11 in front, but alarm bells were ringing for the visitors when, despite having Calum Green in the sin-bin for handling the ball off his feet, Falcons blindside flanker Mark Wilson broke the defensive line to send in impressive full-back Alex Tait for a score to cut the deficit to only four points, with Mike Delany fluffing his second routine conversion of the game.

However, bar a Delany penalty, the final quarter was pretty much all Exeter.

A stunning handling move was finished off in typically fine fashion by James Short, with Steenson adding the extras to give the Chiefs some breathing space.

Then full-back Phil Dollman looked to have grabbed the bonus-point try five minutes from time, but it was referred to the television match official by referee Tim Wigglesworth, and the pictures showed the Welshman had rather embarrassingly lost the ball as he dived over in the corner, injuring himself in the process.

Thankfully, though, Will Chudley spared the Welshman's blushes by attacking the blindside in the dying moments and selling a lovely dummy to squeeze over by the flag to make it a full five-pointer for Exeter against his old club and ensure a very pleasant, but long, coach journey home for the Chiefs.

"Dolly got a fair bit of ribbing for that (from the players and coaching staff) because, when you watch it back, it is almost impossible to see how he didn't score!" laughed Baxter.

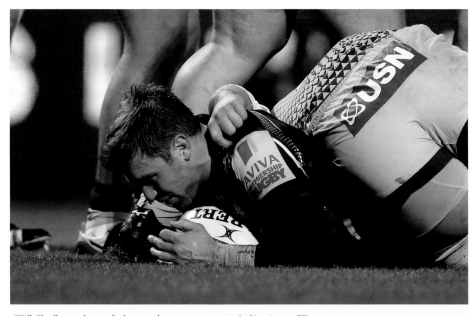

Will Chudley sneaks over for his second try in two games in the big win over Worcester

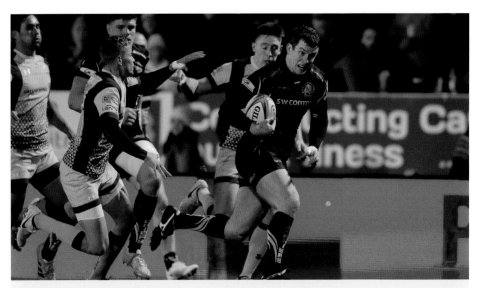

Ian Whitten looks like he has half the Worcester team after him as he races in for a try

"It is interesting how some games give you a bit of an insight into some little things you have got to make sure of. In that case, there is no point trying to slide in, if you can actually just score over the line.

"It was a good learn for the rest of the team, and for Chudders to make up for it was a big moment.

"That was a real, top-quality performance, and any time you go away in the Premiership and get five points, they are genuinely golden moments."

Incredibly, the win lifted Exeter into fourth place in the table, albeit only for 24 hours, but by the end of the weekend they were still fifth, and Newcastle were down in 10th position, showing what a huge difference that victory had made.

Struggling Worcester must have considered a visit to Sandy Park to play an unchanged Exeter team starting to find some good form as the stuff of nightmares.

The Warriors had won only one of their last seven encounters in all competitions – an Anglo-Welsh Cup victory at home to fellow strugglers Bristol – and they had lost all eight previous fixtures against the Chiefs in the Premiership, although they did arrive in Devon off the back of a narrow one-point defeat at home to Northampton, even though they had outscored the Saints 2-0 on tries.

Exeter swept through their visitors like Storm Angus, which had battered the UK during the week leading up to the game, winning the game 57-22, and the Chiefs' ruthless, all-round team display would have made some of their rivals for a top-four place in the Premiership sit up and take note, putting more than 50 points on Worcester for the second time at Sandy Park in only seven months.

Warriors head coach Carl Hogg admitted after the game that his side could not handle Exeter's power and pace, and that the Chiefs' big ball carriers had caused a lot of damage.

A catch-and-drive try from club captain Jack Yeandle, was added to by a sniping effort from Chudley, and a penalty try from another driven line-out, and the bonus point was in the bag early in the second half with a glorious try finished off beside the posts by Olly Woodburn, after great work by Ian Whitten – bursting out of his own 22 – and Chudley.

Further tries followed from Carl Rimmer, Waldrom, Short (after a looped pass from 19-year-old Joe Simmonds, who scored his first Premiership points with a conversion) and Whitten as Exeter delighted the home crowd.

The only black mark was perhaps the three tries they conceded, though two of them came after Waldrom had been yellow carded for a deliberate knock-on.

The Friday-night visit that followed to Sale Sharks, where Exeter had lost the previous two seasons, was the perfect way to truly test out the improvement the Chiefs had made in the previous few weeks.

The match was incredibly refereed once again by Wayne Barnes – the third time he had taken charge of the fixture between the two sides at the AJ Bell Stadium in four seasons.

The Sharks had lost three of their last five home games in all competitions, but the Chiefs had not won successive Premiership away matches in 12 months.

Baxter made six changes to his starting line-up to freshen things up a bit, but the result was much the same as the Chiefs had the game pretty much all sewn up by half-time.

They led 21-3 at the interval, after scoring three converted tries, and that was the scoreline at full-time as well after a pretty dour second half in which both defences were on top.

It was a little frustrating that, having got three tries inside the first 35 minutes, they had failed to score one more for the bonus point in the remaining 45 minutes of the game, but Baxter put that partly down to the difficult conditions in the second period, and did not let that take the gloss off what he felt had been a very satisfying evening's work.

Hooker Yeandle felt the win was based on "a solid set piece, some good decisions from our backs and a lot of kick tennis", and he was also delighted to see the first two scores come from Exeter's driving maul – a major weapon for the Chiefs.

Sale collapsed it on both occasions, with the first leading to a penalty try and a yellow card for Sharks skipper Josh Beaumont, and the second seeing Short squeeze over in the corner for his fourth try in four games, while Barnes was playing a penalty advantage, with Steenson applying the extras to both for a 14-3 lead, with AJ MacGinty slotting a penalty for Sale.

Exeter's third try was much more pleasing on the eye of the neutral, with a beautifully-delayed pass by Short sending centre Sam Hill (who had to change his shirt twice during the game, with blood streaming from a nose injury) clear in midfield. He fed the ball to Chudley racing up on his inside, and he ran the last 25 metres to the line to score his third try in three games. Steenson was once again on the mark with the conversion kick.

Two players who particularly stood out for Exeter on the night were Hill, and back rower Don Armand, who played the full 80 minutes in his first game since September due to injury, and picked up the *BT Sport* man of the match award.

"Hilly did very well. His nose is halfway across his face and he has got a big old hooter anyhow, so it is a lot of nose to squash unfortunately!" said Yeandle.

"Don won man of the match and he justified that and full credit to him, and it shows the work rate that he puts in, and not just the on-the-ball stuff but the off-the-ball stuff as well, and it shows the level of intensity he can bring to a game, and he did very well."

Baxter said it was typical of a man who enjoyed an excellent campaign for the Chiefs.

"Don was the guy who, week in and week out throughout the season, kept his level of performance right up there," said Baxter.

"He is part of our leadership group and he has shown a lot of qualities, both in himself and how he has helped drive the team and pull it forward.

"He became a very important core member of the side in the season, and often players show their top qualities in those awkward games, like Sale away. That's when you need guys to stand up and show great character.

"Often what happens, and in the games we have lost there in the past, guys get a bit frustrated, you give up a silly penalty, they put you in the corner, the maul gets collapsed and then there is a yellow card, and their crowd get going and you start to make silly mistakes. That has been the history of how we have lost there before, but that never looked like being a problem for us this time."

Such was Exeter's defensive effort on the night that it was the fewest number of points Sale had scored in a Premiership home game since their 3-3 draw with Leicester Tigers at their former Edgeley Park pad in February 2004.

"We got it just right that night about what we had to achieve together and individually, and the work we had to put in," said Baxter. "We didn't get the bonus point, but we really didn't give them a sniff in that game.

"If you watched those performances in that block of three, they were based around guys working extremely hard, staying disciplined and being very focused on completing tackles, being good around the clear-out, and being physical in their carries.

"It all sounds very simple, but the players had decided there was no magic to it.

"Just because you had been in a final and finished second in the Premiership, it didn't mean teams were going to roll over in front of you.

"I kind of think a few players, earlier in the season, might have thought that we must be a good team because we had been Premiership runners-up, so things would be okay and eventually a game would go our way, but it doesn't work like that.

"You make everything happen, and I think what you saw in that block of games was us going out there and making things happen.

The players celebrate in the dressing room after picking up Exeter Chiefs' first ever European Champions Cup victory on French soil (picture courtesy of Mark Stevens)

"We went to two traditionally tough places to play in Sale and Newcastle and won. Sale has not been a happy hunting ground for us in the past, and to go there and have as much control physically in the game that we did was a really top quality performance."

The Sale win left Exeter in fifth place in the table, but they were suddenly only one point outside the top four, and had a seven-point cushion over seventh-place Newcastle.

The good news for the Chiefs did not end there either, with Nowell returning from more than two months out with a badly torn quad muscle, picked up in England training, in the A League game against Bath at Sandy Park three days after the Sale fixture.

Exeter headed back into Europe off the back of the three straight Premiership wins and now faced back-to-back matches against Bordeaux-Begles, but their hopes of reaching the knockout stages were all but killed off with a frustrating 13-7 home defeat to the Frenchmen in the first of those two games, which left them with no wins from their opening three pool fixtures.

Jack Maunder's maiden first-team try – following some lovely work by Devoto – converted by Steenson, helped to give the Chiefs a 7-3 lead at the break, and the biggest threat to them winning the game appeared to be the fog rapidly engulfing Sandy Park.

But with the skies clearing, France scrum-half Baptiste Serin scored a try in the second half to add to his first-half penalty, converted by Ireland's Ian Madigan, and a penalty from replacement Lionel Beauxis sealed victory.

A beautiful sunset before fog arrives to put Exeter's home Champions Cup game against Bordeaux-Begles under threat

Lachie Turner twice, and Steenson, had gone so close to further tries for Exeter, while Short controversially had a touchdown ruled out by 2015 World Cup referee Nigel Owens, in consultation with TMO Tim Hayes, who felt he had not grounded the ball under a despairing last-ditch tackle from Marco Tauleigne.

It rather summed up the Chiefs' evening, and Baxter recalled: "Losing the Bordeaux home game was really the deciding factor in us not making it out of our pool.

"I could watch the game back five times and still not really be able to tell you how we lost it, because we had something like 80% possession and 75% territory, and we were on their line about four times and just didn't score, and that created some selection decisions for us for the trip to Bordeaux the following week."

Exeter welcomed back Dollman and Cowan-Dickie from injury in seven changes to the starting line-up for the visit to the Stade Chaban-Delmas, but they came away having made Chiefs' history, with their 20-12 success the first time the club had won a Champions Cup game on French soil.

Their cause was helped by the 49th-minute dismissal of Bordeaux winger Nans Ducuing, when he upended Woodburn in mid-air as they contested a high ball.

Woodburn's landing looked horrible as he came down on his neck and he required treatment, and Irish referee John Lacey had little option but to pull out a red card, much to the fury of the passionate home crowd.

Bordeaux were leading 9-7 at the time, with former French international fly-half Beauxis kicking three penalties for the hosts, to a try by Exeter No.8 Waldrom, converted by Slade.

Beauxis's second first-half penalty had followed a yellow card for Exeter lock Mitch Lees for killing the ball close to his own line, while the Chiefs had also lost back rower Ewers to a tweaked knee injury.

Lacey, who had humorously halted a first-half Exeter attack by accidentally catching the ball, angered the home fans even more by awarding the Chiefs a scrum penalty six minutes after Ducuing's departure, which Slade slotted for a 10-9 lead.

But Bordeaux came storming back, and after Ollie Atkins had put in a try-saving tackle on Louis Madaule, Exeter's replacement prop Greg Holmes was yellow-carded for a tip tackle as the Chiefs continued to make life hard for themselves against 14 men.

Serin's penalty restored Bordeaux's advantage at 12-10, but ten minutes from time, a concerted attack saw Cowan-Dickie – playing his first game in two months – pick up and drive over, with Slade supplying the extras and adding a late penalty to secure victory.

It meant they headed into their final two pool games in January with qualification for the last eight still mathematically possible, albeit very unlikely.

An example of how hard the Exeter coaching team work was demonstrated on that trip when I bumped into forwards coach Rob Hunter walking the streets of Bordeaux just hours after the conclusion of the game.

Instead of celebrating, he was getting some fresh air to clear his mind and start preparing for the following week's big Premiership match against Leicester Tigers in what was to prove another crucial block of fixtures in Exeter's successful Premiership season.

PREMIERSHIP
ROUND 8 – NEWCASTLE FALCONS 19 EXETER CHIEFS 32
(Friday, November 18, Kingston Park)

Newcastle: A Tait; M Watson, D Waldouck, JP Socino, Sinoti Sinoti (V Goneva 61); M Delany (J Hodgson 73), M Young; S Lockwood (R Vickers 55), S Lawson, J Welsh (D Wilson 68); C Green (G Young 68), W Witty; M Wilson, W Welch (capt) (D Nelson 80), A Hogg (O Fonua 68). Replacement (not used): S Egerton.

Chiefs: P Dollman (L Turner 75); O Woodburn, O Devoto, I Whitten, J Short; G Steenson (capt, J Simmonds 79), W Chudley (J Maunder 79); B Moon (C Rimmer 59), J Yeandle (S Malton 79), H Williams (G Holmes 59); M Lees, J Hill (G Parling 63); D Dennis (B White 75), K Horstmann, T Waldrom.

Newcastle: Tries – Lawson, Tait; Penalties – Delany (3).
Exeter: Tries – Devoto, Waldrom, Short, Chudley; Conversions – Steenson (3); Penalties – Steenson (2).

Yellow Card: Newcastle – Green.

HT: 8-14. **Referee:** Tim Wigglesworth (RFU). **Attendance:** 8,061.

ROUND 9

EXETER CHIEFS 57 WORCESTER WARRIORS 22

(Saturday, November 26, Sandy Park)

Chiefs: P Dollman (S Hill 34); O Woodburn, O Devoto, I Whitten, J Short; G Steenson (capt, J Simmonds 56), W Chudley (J Maunder 50); B Moon (C Rimmer 49), J Yeandle (S Malton 50), H Williams (G Holmes 49); M Lees (G Parling 58), J Hill; D Dennis, K Horstmann (D Ewers 56), T Waldrom.

Worcester: C Pennell (T Biggs 64); B Heem (J Willison 51), D Hammond, W Olivier, J Adams; J Shillcock, J Arr (M Dowsett 15-19, 46); V Rapava Ruskin (N Leleimalefaga 51), J Singleton (M Williams 72), N Schonert (M Daniels 58); A Kitchener, D Barry (D O'Callaghan 62); D Potgieter, C Kirwan (S Lewis 46), P Dowson (capt).

Exeter: Tries – Yeandle, Chudley, penalty try, Woodburn, Rimmer, Waldrom, Short, Whitten; Conversions – Steenson (6), J Simmonds; Penalty – Steenson.
Worcester: Tries – Adams, Olivier, Potgieter; Conversions – Shillcock (2); Penalty – Shillcock.

Yellow Cards: Exeter – Waldrom; Worcester – Barry.

HT: 24-3. **Referee:** Matthew O'Grady (RFU). **Attendance:** 11,055.

ROUND 10 – SALE SHARKS 3 EXETER CHIEFS 21

(Friday, December 2, AJ Bell Stadium)

Sale: M Haley (P Odogwu 78); T Arscott, S James, J Leota, J Charnley; AJ MacGinty (S Tuitupou 67), M Phillips (P Stringer 46); R Harrison (J Flynn 70), R Webber (N Briggs 60), B Mujati (H Aulika 50); B Evans, J Beaumont (capt); C Neild, B Curry (D Seymour 50), TJ Ioane (J Mills 61).

Chiefs: L Turner; O Woodburn, O Devoto, S Hill (M Campagnaro 30-33, 67), J Short; G Steenson (capt), W Chudley; C Rimmer (B Moon 52), J Yeandle (S Malton 78), G Holmes (H Williams 52); M Lees (J Hill 59), G Parling; D Armand, K Horstmann (D Ewers 60), T Waldrom. Replacements (not used): J Maunder, J Simmonds.

Sale: Penalty – MacGinty.
Chiefs: Tries – penalty try, Short, Chudley; Conversions – Steenson (3).

Yellow Cards: Sale – Beaumont. Exeter – Campagnaro.

HT: 3-21. **Referee:** Wayne Barnes (RFU). **Attendance:** 4,479.

EUROPEAN CHAMPIONS CUP

ROUND 3 – EXETER CHIEFS 7 BORDEAUX-BEGLES 13

(Sunday, December 11, Sandy Park)

Chiefs: L Turner; J Nowell, O Devoto (M Campagnaro 76), H Slade (S Hill 62), J Short; G Steenson (capt), J Maunder (W Chudley 54); B Moon (C Rimmer 54),J Yeandle (S Malton 76), T Francis (G Holmes 54); G Parling (O Atkins 43), J Hill; D Ewers, D Armand, D Dennis (K Horstmann 62).

Bordeaux-Begles: J-M Buttin; N Ducuing (J Vakacegu 66), R Lonca, J Rey, B Connor; I Madigan (L Beauxis 60), B Serin (capt) (Y Lesgourgues 57); S Kitshoff (S Taofifenua 51), O Avei (C Maynadier 51), M Clerc (J-B Poux 51); T Palmer (L Jones ht), B Botha; L Goujon, J Edwards (H Chalmers 51), M Tauleigne.

Chiefs: Try – Maunder; Conversion – Steenson.
Bordeaux: Try – Serin; Conversion – Madigan; Penalties – Serin, Beauxis.

HT: 7-3. **Referee:** Nigel Owens (Wales). **Attendance:** 9,143.

ROUND 4 – BORDEAUX-BEGLES 12 EXETER CHIEFS 20

(Saturday, December 17, Stade Chaban-Delmas)

Bordeaux-Begles: G Cros; N Ducuing, R Lonca (J-M Buttin 70), J Vakacegu, J-B Dubie; L Beauxis (B Serin 62), J Audy (G Doubrere 50); S Taofifenua (X Civil 63), O Avei (B Auzqui 63), M Clerc (J-B Poux 55); T Palmer, B Botha (C Cazeaux 62); L Goujon (capt), J Edwards (L Madaule 33), M Tauleigne.

Chiefs: P Dollman; J Nowell, I Whitten, S Hill (M Campagnaro 61), O Woodburn; H Slade, W Chudley (J Maunder 55); C Rimmer (M Low 55), L Cowan-Dickie (S Malton 74), H Williams (G Holmes 49); M Lees, O Atkins (D Dennis 59); D Ewers (D Armand 30), K Horstmann (capt), T Waldrom (H Williams 71-74). Replacement (not used): J Simmonds.

Bordeaux: Penalties – Beauxis (3), Serin.
Chiefs: Tries – Waldrom, Cowan-Dickie; Conversions – Slade (2); Penalties – Slade (2).

Red Card: Bordeaux – Ducuing. **Yellow Cards:** Chiefs – Lees, Holmes.

HT: 6-7. **Referee:** John Lacey (Ireland). **Attendance:** 21,071.

Gareth Steenson demonstrates a finely-honed technique that any young kicker should learn from – keeping your head down after you have struck the ball in the game at Saracens

CHAPTER 6

The Perfect Christmas

PREMIERSHIP TABLE							
	P	W	D	L	F	A	Pts
Wasps	13	11	0	2	415	277	51
Saracens	13	10	1	2	312	147	48
EXETER	**13**	**7**	**2**	**4**	**337**	**239**	**41**
Bath	13	8	0	5	294	216	38
Leicester	13	7	0	6	285	265	33
Northampton	13	7	0	6	239	235	33
Harlequins	13	7	0	6	280	311	32
Gloucester	13	4	2	7	319	277	30
Newcastle	13	6	0	7	228	315	29
Sale	13	3	1	9	245	322	20
Worcester	13	2	2	9	234	409	14
Bristol	13	2	0	11	216	391	13

DECEMBER

Saturday 24	AP	W	Exeter Chiefs 31	Leicester Tigers 10
Saturday 31	AP	W	Bath 11	Exeter Chiefs 17

JANUARY

Saturday 7	AP	D	Saracens 13	Exeter Chiefs 13
Sunday 15	ECC	W	Exeter Chiefs 31	Ulster 19
Saturday 21	ECC	L	Clermont Auvergne 48	Exeter Chiefs 26
Saturday 28	AWC	W	Exeter Chiefs 52	Wasps 5

FEBRUARY

Sunday 5	AWC	W	Bristol 7	Exeter Chiefs 35

Premiership points available 15 – points taken 11

CHRISTMAS could not get much better from an Exeter Chiefs point of view than a 31-10 bonus-point win over Leicester Tigers at Sandy Park to leapfrog the Midlanders into fourth spot.

That was quite a remarkable league position to be in on Christmas Eve, given the Chiefs' indifferent start to the campaign. It meant their hopes of a play-off place were now in their own hands, and they were to remain in the top four for the rest of the season.

It was widely expected to be a very tight game, with Exeter going into the contest with only one defeat in six matches in all competitions, and the Tigers one loss in seven, but the match was all but over by the break as the Chiefs led 21-0 following a dominant first-half display.

It was only their second victory over the Midlanders in nine Premiership games.

It was results like this that led to the sacking, only two days into the New Year, of Tigers' long-standing director of rugby Richard Cockerill, a person who Rob Baxter has a lot of respect for and has always got on very well with.

The tone for Exeter's display was set by England international winger Jack Nowell – making only his second Premiership appearance of the season – with an electrifying break straight from the kick-off that saw him rip through the heart of Leicester's midfield.

Exeter used their driving maul to lethal effect, kicking any penalties they had to the corner, and it served up tries for Jack Yeandle and Thomas Waldrom, against his old club.

They were also awarded a penalty try – that would end the season as Exeter's joint fourth top try scorer in the Premiership with six – when Graham Kitchener was adjudged to have deliberately knocked on when Olly Woodburn was lurking on the wing to take a pass from Will Chudley until the Leicester lock's intervention, and was rightly sin-binned for his misdemeanour.

Gareth Steenson converted all three and the Chiefs were in dream world with a 21-point half-time advantage, which was extended by three more points by a penalty from the Irishman early in the second half.

The 10-times Premiership champions fought their way back, and after Ed Slater had dropped the ball over the try line following an excellent last-ditch tackle by the magnificent Nowell, back rower Brendon O'Connor dived over for their first points of the game with a touchdown from a close-range ruck.

Exeter responded in typical fashion though, with Ollie Devoto claiming his first try in Exeter colours at Sandy Park, after good work by wingers James Short and Woodburn, to wrap up the bonus point, with Steenson adding the extras.

There was still time for a late consolation score from Jono Kitto, but the Tigers were well beaten.

"I thought we played really well against Leicester," admitted Baxter. "You could start to see in that game what we were talking about, and what actually feels right.

Exeter head coach Rob Baxter was not too critical of his players after their draw at reigning Premiership champions Saracens

"We had a scrum that went forward, and a maul that went forward – that feels right, especially when you do it against a side like Leicester.

"I remember our scrum being particularly good that day. There have been plenty of games in our time in the Premiership where we have started to feel squeezed by Leicester's set piece, and it feels very difficult for you to get into the game.

"It didn't feel so difficult to get into that game on Christmas Eve because our set piece stood up, our forwards stood up, and that created a huge platform for us that we were really able to exploit.

"It was one of those games where you could feel we were getting to where we wanted to be."

The Exeter fans were very satisfied with that success over the Tigers, but for the Chiefs to then back that up by getting their first ever Premiership win at the Recreation Ground against old rivals Bath really was the stuff of dreams over the festive period, although they had triumphed there before in an LV= Cup semi-final in March 2014 on their way to lifting the trophy against Northampton Saints at Sandy Park.

It was the first time Exeter had won four successive games away from home in all competitions in the same season since the 2011-12 campaign.

They went into the sell-out match having made one enforced change, with Henry Slade ruled out with a neck/shoulder injury, and they were eager to exact revenge for their Sandy Park defeat to Bath only two months before, when they went down to Semesa Rokoduguni's late, late try.

However, after an hour, it looked like it was going to be the usual Chiefs story at The Rec, with Bath dominating proceedings and leading 11-0.

Rokoduguni was causing mayhem in the Chiefs' ranks, and he was only denied one first-half try by a superb tackle from Nowell.

However, he did manage to cross the whitewash before the break, and added to two George Ford penalties, Bath had a comfortable interval advantage, and Exeter were in for an uncharacteristic dressing down from Baxter at half-time.

It was the only Chiefs' Premiership game I had missed all season, as I was away on a family holiday in the Lake District (yes, several comedians have already suggested I should permanently stay away from Bath when Chiefs are playing there!), and Paddy Marsh, who was commentating for *BBC Radio Devon* that day in my absence, had just asked the question of 'when was the last time Exeter had failed to score a single point in a Premiership game?' (the answer is never), when the comeback began.

Steenson slotted a 62nd minute penalty from 40 metres to get the Chiefs' first points on the board, but even then they were indebted to a try-saving tackle by Phil Dollman on England winger Anthony Watson – a score that would have surely wrapped the game up in Bath's favour.

Instead, the Chiefs produced a flurry of attacking waves, and with only eight minutes remaining, Luke Cowan-Dickie powered his way through the Bath defence, juggling with the ball in the process before finger-tipping it away to Short, who raced over in the left-hand corner.

Steenson kicked a wonderful touchline conversion, and Exeter were suddenly within a point of their rivals.

The drama was not done though. Nowell went on a mazy run before the forwards drove possession up to the line.

The chance for a score looked lost when the ball flew out of a ruck, but the quick-thinking Steenson brilliantly scooped it between his legs into the arms of the waiting Short, lurking out on the wing, who sneaked in for his second try in six minutes, and with only three minutes left on the clock.

The Exeter Chiefs Supporters' Club would later vote it the Champagne Moment of the Season.

Steenson again added the extras, and the final whistle blew soon after to signal the start of some wonderful New Year celebrations for the Devon side and their supporters.

Exeter were now third in the table, with a match against second-place Saracens, the reigning European and Premiership champions, to come the following week.

"The Christmas period was fantastic for us, and that's the kind of one you want as a coach and a player," said Baxter.

"To be able to play on Christmas Eve in front of a bumper crowd, and then let your players get away and have Christmas Day and Boxing Day off, and then bring them back in and have a relatively short journey to Bath for our next match.

"The most satisfying thing for me about the Bath game was not actually that we had played that well, because for large periods of the match we were not playing to our potential, but you could just see character dripping out of the players in that second half.

"It was interesting because I don't often challenge the players in a forceful way too much, because they are a good set of guys, but it was one of the few games I did that. I remember saying to them at half-time: 'Is this as much as we are going to put into the game? Are we really going to walk away from here and say we are happy with this level of performance?

"'Rokoduguni is not wearing an invisibility cloak, you ARE allowed to tackle him. What is going on out there? He is a good player but you are making him look like an absolute world beater. Come on, if you lay hands on him you can tackle him. Let's start driving the positives and let's start driving ourselves here'.

"People said we were perhaps a bit fortuitous with the scrum situation and them starting to pick up front-row injuries, but the majority of the attritional side of a game is what you are prepared to make it, and if you really start driving yourself physically, a lot of the attrition issues the opposition have are created by you through pressure, and I think that is very much what we did in the second half.

Exeter Chiefs

"Bath probably should have been further ahead in the first half, but they weren't, and they left an opportunity for us.

"We played some good rugby in the second half, and I can only really remember one spell of pressure from Bath in that period, and other than that it was about us pouring it on.

"Eventually we got the scores that mattered and a fantastically satisfying win away at Bath.

"When you look back at that match, and then how close we were, by the end of the season, to not getting a home semi-final, you realise how important games like that were.

"But what we did really well was keeping things in our own hands and not letting things get taken off us easily, and I think the Bath game is a perfect example of that."

The two Short tries – which took him to six in seven games – were both memorable for different reasons, and Baxter said: "They come in funny ways, don't they?

"You could say Luke was losing that ball for Shorty's first try and managed to get away with it, but a lot of those little moments that went for us, I think they are the perfect example of things going your way because you are getting your intensity levels right.

"We've lost plenty of tight games, and normally you can put your finger on the fact that you have dropped off the intensity levels you need to be at for a brief moment.

"You look at the home game with Bath, we had a lazy scrum around about halfway, which Bath managed to disrupt and win a penalty, and they put the ball into the corner.

"We then realised we were under a bit of pressure and scrummaged quite well and managed to get them to play the ball away, and we defended the initial threat really well, and were driving them up the field, and it actually looked like we were back in control, but then two guys missed a tackle that should never really get missed and Rokoduguni scored a try that won Bath the game.

"Some people will say it is great play from Bath, but I am prepared to say it was us dropping off the intensity levels we needed, not focusing on our set piece, and then not focusing defensively for the fourth or fifth phase.

"In the game away to Bath, we probably weren't playing with the intensity we needed, but we did something about that during the game, and you can then see what happened to Bath when they dropped off the intensity levels they needed.

"Fortune tends to favour the team playing on the edge and playing at the levels needed, and I think we saw that on numerous occasions during the season."

Could the Chiefs now make it an incredible three wins out of three against sides in the top four in the table by beating second-place Saracens on their own Allianz Park pitch?

Sarries went into the game matching Exeter's one-defeat-in-eight record, and having not lost on their own patch in any competition in 10 months.

Jack Nowell scores a wonderful try at Allianz Park against Saracens, avoiding the clutches of Richard Wigglesworth

They had won their three matches against the Chiefs the previous season, including the Twickenham final, and also managed that comfortable victory at Sandy Park on the second weekend of this campaign.

Baxter freshened up his side, making six changes in the pack, including a first Premiership start in 12 months for former England back rower Tom Johnson and handing places in the back division to Short and the fit-again Slade.

Sarries were missing England quintet Owen Farrell, Chris Ashton, George Kruis and the Vunipola brothers, Mako and Billy, but it was still a very strong starting XV and they had five full internationals on their bench.

It was a milestone match for their Devon-born loose-head prop Richard Barrington, a former Okehampton player, but it was one that would be remembered for so much more than his 100th appearance for the club.

His game lasted only 11 minutes before he was red-carded by referee Ian Tempest after he was deemed to have led with his shoulder into a tackle that knocked out Exeter's former England lock Geoff Parling.

What Tempest and television match official Sean Davey inexplicably missed, despite looking at the footage, was that Parling's head connected with Barrington's shoulder as a result of a high, swinging forearm from Sarries captain Brad Barritt.

When the skipper was beckoned over by the referee, he no doubt expected his game to be over, but instead it was Barrington who was sent off, with Tempest apologising to the forward for having to dismiss him.

The moment of impact for Geoff Parling on Devon-born Saracens prop Richard Barrington's shoulder, as he is tackled high by home skipper Brad Barritt, is brilliantly captured by Tom Sandberg. Barritt's expression as referee Ian Tempest shows Barrington a red card says it all

Not surprisingly, when the Rugby Football Union disciplinary chiefs reviewed the footage three days later, Barrington was cleared of any wrongdoing, while Barritt was handed a three-week ban for a dangerous tackle.

Exeter controlled the opening 40 minutes in front of a capacity crowd but only led 10-3 at the break.

Don Armand on his way to the try line against Saracens, but the ball was dislodged on contact as he crossed the whitewash

Steenson landed a penalty and converted a stunning try by Nowell, who plucked the Irishman's crossfield kick out of the air with one hand and dotted down all in one movement.

It was a moment of Lions class from Nowell, who was a surprise inclusion by the Chiefs, given that he usually misses matches on artificial pitches, due to his long-standing knee problems.

Baxter explained afterwards: "We are continually trying to strengthen Jack and get him to a position where he can train more often, and he can load heavier and he can play on these kinds of surfaces.

"It is going to be a bit-by-bit battle. It is not going to be something that just happens overnight. We have had to manage Jack extremely carefully, and as his knee strengthens, and when he is in good nick after a period of rest, we do have the opportunity to occasionally play him on this surface."

Alex Lozowski kicked a penalty for Sarries, but the Chiefs thought they had scored again right on the stroke of half-time, when Don Armand galloped clear and was heading for the line, only to lose the ball in contact from Saracens duo Chris Wyles and Michael Rhodes as he tried to ground it.

Lozowski slotted another penalty, and Steenson missed a chance of his own before adding a three-pointer to make it 13-6 to the Chiefs, but the hosts levelled matters with a catch-and-drive try by big replacement prop Titi Lamositele, converted by Lozowski, with only four minutes remaining.

Exeter had one last chance to snatch victory, with a late Steenson drop-goal attempt, but they had to settle for a share of the spoils.

"It sounds strange, but the red card almost suited them more than it did us," recalled Baxter.

"We were playing really well and going at them with some really good intensity, and I actually felt like we had them rattled.

"Then we had the red card, which could easily have been two reds – and it turned out it had been given to the wrong player after the citing procedure had been completed – and it solidified Saracens.

"They said: 'We are going to stick with eight forwards, and make it this kind of a game', and to be fair to them, even though it took them until quite late in the game to get the levelling score, you have to give them great credit for how they dealt with it.

> We were playing really well and going at them with some really good intensity, and I actually felt like we had them rattled

"I wasn't too critical of the lads after the game and said to them: 'The annoying thing is you have actually played pretty well and done most things quite well, and all people are going to talk about is Saracens coming through and getting a draw with 14 men'.

"We talked about Saracens, and the fact they had shown some good qualities and that you can weather these storms and deal with going down to 14 men.

"The major thing we talked about going into that game was the intensity we wanted to show in the opening period, and we wanted to hit that pitch ready to play in a way that was going to challenge Saracens.

"We kept it really simple that week, and we achieved our goal, so I wasn't going to sit in the changing room after we had got a draw away from home in the Premiership and try and find all kinds of ways to be critical.

"Did we get everything perfectly right and take all our opportunities? No, we didn't, but we went there with a game plan that challenged Saracens and put them under pressure, they made some uncharacteristic mistakes, we scored some points, and even though we didn't see the game out, it was still a good learn for us.

"We were still ticking along, we were in the top four and still progressing as a team, and a lot of teams go to Saracens and don't get anything, and we did okay and it certainly didn't dent us at all.

"It gave us confidence when we came to the semi-final in how we wanted to play against Saracens, and the qualities we needed to show, and even though it was a draw, huge parts of that game were a massive bonus for us."

It could not have been a tougher run of fixtures for the Chiefs, but they had come through it with an amazing 11 points out of a possible 15.

It was around this time that I said to my wife that I firmly believed Baxter felt he had a team that could, and possibly would, win the Premiership at the end of the season.

It is not something he would have ever said publicly at that time, and it might sound a bit naff, but having interviewed him hundreds of times before and after games down through the years, I thought I could sense that steely inner belief when I spoke to him.

Interviewing him for this book six weeks after the final had been won, he agreed that was fair comment.

"That came from watching the players train, seeing how they talked and how they played," he explained.

"I have said on a fair few occasions to Ali Hepher in the time he has been at the club, when I sit down and talk to the players and look at the good qualities and good characteristics that they show most of the time, I genuinely don't feel we are a team that is going to get relegated, because I feel we have got a group of guys who will drag us through some pretty awful situations.

"To start the season relatively poorly and then put ourselves into a position to win the Premiership was not actually what I meant!

"The players were honest enough to admit they were not driving the season and they were kind of waiting for it to take off, and once as a group they decided to drive the season, instead of almost waiting to see if someone was going to ignite it, and some great performance was going to happen, and it would all click into place – which to be fair does happen with some teams – I was confident that a decent season was on its way and we would give ourselves a chance of winning the league.

"My approach to coaching has very much been to try and prepare a team in a way that gives itself as many opportunities as possible to put in a good performance and win a game.

"That will ultimately lead to a higher percentage of wins, and one thing leads to another.

"It very rarely felt like a fantastic season because of the start we made. Because of the trials we had gone through as a group in that first third of the season, it felt like we were chasing things down, which in a way suited us because we were going after things week by week, which worked very well for us.

"We were showing some really good fighting qualities, and it did start to feel like we had something special happening."

Before the Premiership resumed again more than a month later, the Chiefs were fighting on two more fronts in cup competitions.

First, was the small matter of finishing off their Champions Cup pool, with Ulster at Sandy Park, followed by another trip to Clermont Auvergne's fantastic Stade Marcel Michelin.

Even though it was the third time Exeter had been there in five years, you could never tire of visiting one of the best club rugby grounds in Europe.

The Sarries game took its toll on Chudley, with a torn pectoral muscle ruling him out of action until the penultimate game of the league season against Northampton, while

Jack Nowell's head-to-head with Charles Piutau was a fascinating sideshow in the match against Ulster

Thomas Waldrom celebrates his try against Ulster in typical Thomas the Tank Engine 'Toot, Toot' style!

dreadfully unlucky prop Alec Hepburn ruptured an anterior cruciate ligament during a game of touch rugby in training on his return from a broken thumb.

Chudley's absence meant a first start in more than two months for Dave Lewis in the number nine shirt, while youngster Stu Townsend was named on the bench as cover.

Italian international Michele Campagnaro scores one of his two tries against Ulster in the Champions Cup in a man-of-the-match display

This block of cup games will best be remembered for the emergence of Italian international centre Michele Campagnaro, who rapidly became a huge fans' favourite at Sandy Park.

He was in his second season at Sandy Park, and I had been saying on *BBC Radio Devon* for 18 months that he had the potential to become one of Rob Baxter's best ever signings, but I never believed he would fulfil that potential with Exeter.

That was because he was either missing through international duty, was out injured, or when he was fit, trying to break into a midfield that had so much talent in it, with the likes of Henry Slade, Sam Hill, Ollie Devoto and Ian Whitten all seemingly ahead of him in the pecking order, appeared to be an impossible task.

However, he was given only his second start of the season against Ulster, and in the next three games he bagged six tries, before heading off once again on international duty.

His two against Ulster in a man-of-the-match display were equalled by a double from Thomas Waldrom in one of those memorable European fixtures at Sandy Park, sitting on a par with famous wins over Cardiff Blues (2013), Clermont Auvergne (2015) and Ospreys (2016).

The Ulster game itself though will remain long in the memory for one of the best head-to-head battles ever witnessed at Sandy Park, between Exeter's Jack Nowell and Ulster's former New Zealand All Blacks ace Charles Piutau, who bagged two tries.

"It was as good as it is going to get, with winger against winger, and they both showed what really good players they are in what was a fantastic game," said Baxter.

"You would pay a fortune to have them both in the same team.

"Our approach to the match was relatively simple, and we talked about making it a real game of character, and showing the type of team we could be in the Champions Cup.

"A win for Ulster, with a home game against Bordeaux to come the week after, would have left the battle for runners-up spot in their hands.

"We had been a bit frustrated with a couple of things that had happened in Europe during the season, and by then we were the kind of animal that was working out what we needed to do, individually as much as collectively.

"It was just one of those really good European days, and it was frustrating it didn't lead to more for us, but when you look at how the season panned out, it was still an important process for us to go through with regards to the qualities we could show, and how good we could be when we got things right."

Exeter also notched a penalty try, with Steenson adding three conversions, in a cracking Sunday evening contest – the third time in three home Champions Cup matches the Chiefs had been handed the 5.30pm graveyard slot on the Sabbath by television companies – much to the annoyance of Exeter chairman and chief executive Tony Rowe OBE, who made his feelings known to European rugby bosses.

Clermont had sealed top spot in the group even before the Exeter-Ulster game had kicked off, with a narrow, uninspiring win in Bordeaux earlier in the afternoon.

But the Chiefs' victory lifted them into second place in the pool and meant they still had an outside chance of finishing as one of the best three runners-up in the five groups.

To do so they needed at least a bonus-point victory in Clermont, and for other results to go their way, but there was every chance the Frenchmen might field a weakened team, having already qualified for the last eight.

That 'every chance' became a 'fat chance' as they instead wheeled out the heavy artillery to face the Chiefs as they were desperate to clinch the number one seeding to give them a home quarter-final and the best chance of progressing through the knockout stages.

Exeter's European dream was pretty much over after only nine minutes, with tries by Benjamin Kayser and Noa Nakaitaci giving Clermont a 12-0 lead.

Three more touchdowns had followed by the break as the hosts moved gloriously through the gears in a half in which the Chiefs had been reduced to 13 men by the controversial sin-binning of winger Olly Woodburn and centre Ollie Devoto in the space of only three minutes by Irish referee Andrew Brace.

The half-time score of 34-0 became 34-7 only 51 seconds into the second period when Devoto broke from deep inside his own half, Maunder continued the move and Short finished off, but normal service was swiftly resumed by Clermont – who had lost France centre Wesley Fofana to a season-ending injury in the 37th minute – with two more converted tries to make it 48-7.

It was certainly a case of after the horse had bolted, but Exeter still deserved enormous credit for the way they kept going to score three more touchdowns in an amazing eight-minute spell to secure a four-try bonus point, with Devoto, Woodburn and Campagnaro all crossing.

Europe was over for another season for Exeter, but they still had strong hopes of making progress in the Anglo-Welsh Cup, and the boot was quickly on the other foot as they crushed a very weak Wasps side 52-5 at Sandy Park in round three of the pool stages.

Under-18 starlet Joe Snow made his first-team debut off the bench, while Will Hooley and Matt Jess returned from injury – the latter out with a significant toe problem he picked up playing for the Braves in their A League game away to Saracens in September.

The indefatigable Campagnaro, playing on the wing rather than in the centre, stole the headlines again with a hat-trick as the Chiefs ran in eight tries, with two for the hosts and one by Wasps' Will Rowlands coming in a chaotic opening 10 minutes.

Young back rower Sam Simmonds scored arguably the try of the match with a tremendous burst of pace off a line-out move and a wonderful sidestep around the last defender.

Exeter, skippered by young Sam Skinner, led 33-5 at the break, and they piled on the agony in the second half to rack up a further 19 points.

It was a great win, but no-one was reading anything into this demolition job ahead of the visit of the Premiership-leading Wasps first team a fortnight later.

Having put themselves in pole position in the group with this victory, albeit only ahead of Ospreys on points difference, Exeter duly booked their place in the last four eight days later with a bonus-point 35-7 win at Bristol.

Sam Simmonds scorches his way through the Wasps defence to grab a touchdown in their Anglo-Welsh Cup clash

Exeter Chiefs

Young lock Sam Skinner skippered the Chiefs to a place in the Anglo-Welsh Cup semi-finals with victory over Bristol

However, they had to keep a keen eye on the Ospreys game against Wasps taking place at the Ricoh Arena the same afternoon to make sure of their semi-final spot. The Welshmen won 31-22 but it was not enough to deny Exeter.

Henry Slade was released from the England camp to play in the Bristol game, while Australian flanker Julian Salvi got his first taste of action since suffering a bicep injury against Ulster in Belfast in October.

Two penalty tries and further scores from Shaun Malton, Slade and Max Bodilly, all converted by Joe Simmonds, earned the Chiefs a home semi-final against Harlequins, but thoughts of that were put firmly on the back burner as they prepared for a massive match on their return to Premiership action.

Max Bodilly on his way to one of five tries in the Anglo-Welsh Cup win at Bristol

PREMIERSHIP

ROUND 11 – EXETER CHIEFS 31 LEICESTER TIGERS 10

(Saturday, December 24, Sandy Park)

Chiefs: P Dollman; J Nowell (J Short 64-72), O Devoto, H Slade (S Hill 28), O Woodburn (J Short 72); G Steenson (capt), W Chudley (J Maunder 68); B Moon (C Rimmer 62), J Yeandle (L Cowan-Dickie 56), T Francis (G Holmes 56), M Lees, J Hill (O Atkins 62); D Dennis (K Horstmann 60), D Armand, T Waldrom.

Leicester: F Burns (G Worth 68); A Thompstone, J Roberts, M Tuilagi, P Betham; O Williams, S Harrison (J Kitto 64); E Genge (L Mulipola 67, Genge 72), G McGuigan (H Thacker 56), P Cilliers (D Cole 45); E Slater (capt), M Fitzgerald; M Williams (G Kitchener 23), B O'Connor, L Hamilton (W Evans 68). Replacement (not used): T Brady.

Chiefs: Tries – Yeandle, Waldrom, penalty try, Devoto; Conversions – Steenson (4); Penalty – Steenson.
Leicester: Tries – O'Connor, Kitto.

HT: 21-0. **Referee:** Tom Foley (RFU). **Attendance:** 12,420.

ROUND 12 – BATH 11 EXETER CHIEFS 17

(Saturday, December 31, Recreation Ground)

Bath: T Homer; S Rokoduguni, J Joseph, B Tapuai (M Clark 78), A Brew (A Watson 52); G Ford, K Fotuali'i; N Catt (N Auterac 18, M Van Vuuren 61-74), T Dunn, M Lahiff (S Knight 36); M Garvey (capt, E Stooke 62), D Attwood; T Ellis, F Louw (P Grant 66), Z Mercer. Replacements (not used): D Allinson, A Watson.

Chiefs: P Dollman; J Nowell, O Devoto, S Hill, O Woodburn (J Short 52); G Steenson (capt), W Chudley (J Maunder 62); B Moon (C Rimmer 50), J Yeandle (L Cowan-Dickie 50), T Francis (G Holmes 50); M Lees, J Hill (O Atkins 63); D Dennis (K Horstmann 60), D Armand, T Waldrom. Replacement (not used): J Simmonds.

Bath: Try – Rokoduguni; Penalties – Ford (2).
Chiefs: Tries – Short (2); Conversions – Steenson (2); Penalty – Steenson.

HT: 11-0. **Referee:** Craig Maxwell-Keys (RFU). **Attendance:** 14,509.

ROUND 13 – SARACENS 13 EXETER CHIEFS 13

(Saturday, January 7, Allianz Park)

Saracens: A Goode; S Maitland (T Lamositele 14), M Bosch (N Tompkins 5, D Taylor 53, B Spencer 70), B Barritt (capt), C Wyles; A Lozowski, R Wigglesworth; R Barrington, S Brits (J George 51), J Figallo (V Koch 49); M Itoje, J Hamilton; M Rhodes (W Skelton 51), K Brown (S Burger 62), J Wray.

Chiefs: P Dollman; J Nowell, S Hill, H Slade (I Whitten 63), J Short; G Steenson (capt), W Chudley (J Maunder 65); C Rimmer (B Moon 49), L Cowan-Dickie (J Yeandle 53), G Holmes (H Williams 49); O Atkins (D Dennis 45), G Parling (M Lees 11); D Armand, T Johnson, T Waldrom. Replacement (not used): M Campagnaro.

Saracens: Try – Lamositele; Conversion – Lozowski; Penalties – Lozowski (2).
Chiefs: Try –Nowell; Conversion – Steenson; Penalties – Steenson (2).

Red Card: Saracens – Barrington.

HT: 3-10. **Referee:** Ian Tempest (RFU). **Attendance:** 10,000.

CHAMPIONS CUP

ROUND 5 – EXETER CHIEFS 31 ULSTER 19

(Sunday, January 15, Sandy Park)

Chiefs: P Dollman; J Nowell, M Campagnaro, I Whitten (O Devoto 64), O Woodburn; G Steenson (capt), D Lewis (S Townsend 67); B Moon (M Low 60), L Cowan-Dickie (J Yeandle 60), G Holmes (H Williams 60); M Lees, J Hill (D Dennis 64); T Johnson (K Horstmann 54), D Armand, T Waldrom. Replacement (not used): J Simmonds.

Ulster: L Ludik; C Piutau, L Marshall (J Stockdale 61), S McCloskey, A Trimble (capt, B Herron 73); P Jackson, D Shanahan (P Marshall 77); C Black (A Warwick 46), R Best (J Andrew 77), R Kane (J Simpson 34); K Treadwell (F Van Der Merwe 64), P Browne (C Ross 54); I Henderson, C Henry, S Reidy.

Chiefs: Tries – Campagnaro (2), Waldrom (2), penalty try; Conversions – Steenson (3).
Ulster: Tries – Reidy, Piutau (2); Conversions – Jackson (2).

Yellow Card: Ulster – Jackson.

HT: 12-12. **Referee:** Romain Poite (Fra). **Attendance:** 10,671.

ROUND 6

CLERMONT AUVERGNE 48 EXETER CHIEFS 26

(Saturday, January 21, Stade Marcel Michelin)

Clermont: S Spedding (A Raka 71); N Nakaitaci, R Lamerat, W Fofana (A Rougerie 37), N Abendanon; C Lopez, M Parra (capt, L Radosavljevic 51); R Chaume (V Debaty 54), B Kayser (J Ulugia 54), A Jarvis (D Zirakashvili 54); A Iturria (P Jedrasik 71), S Vahaamahina; P Yato, A Lapandry, F Lee (D Chouly 52).

Chiefs: P Dollman; O Woodburn, M Campagnaro, O Devoto, J Short (I Whitten 62); G Steenson (capt, J Simmonds 62), J Maunder (S Townsend 58); B Moon (M Low 54), J Yeandle (L Cowan-Dickie 54), T Francis (H Williams 54); O Atkins (D Welch 49), J Hill; D Armand (T Johnson 36), K Horstmann, T Waldrom.

Clermont: Tries – Kayser, Nakaitaci, penalty try, Fofana, Abendanon, Yato, Lapandry; Conversions – Parra (5); Penalty – Parra.
Chiefs: Tries – Short, Devoto, Woodburn, Campagnaro; Conversions – Steenson (2), Simmonds.

Yellow Cards: Chiefs - Woodburn, Devoto.

HT: 34-0. **Referee:** Andrew Brace (Ireland). **Attendance:** 17,201.

ANGLO-WELSH CUP

ROUND 3 – EXETER CHIEFS 52 WASPS 5

(Saturday, January 28, Sandy Park)

Chiefs: L Turner; M Campagnaro, M Bodilly (M Jess 61), S Hill (T Lawday 69), J Short; J Simmonds (W Hooley 63), S Townsend (J Snow 65); C Rimmer (M Low 59), S Malton (J Innard 59), T Francis (J Owlett 59); M Lees (G Parling 55), D Welch; S Skinner (capt), B White, S Simmonds.

Wasps: P O'Conor (J Hodson 59); G Armitage, N De Luca (capt), B Macken, T Howe; J Umaga (W Seals 51), C Hampson (W Porter 67); T Bristow (T West 55, T Bristow 74), K Britton, W Stuart (S McIntyre 51); W Rowland (A Johnson 76), M Garratt (E Ehizode 71); A Bone (J Willis 74), J Willis (T Willis 67), A Rieder.

Chiefs: Tries – Campagnaro (3), Lees, Malton, S Simmonds, Townsend, Turner; Conversions – J Simmonds (6).
Wasps: Try – Rowlands.

HT: 33-5. **Referee:** Greg Macdonald (RFU). **Attendance:** 10,551.

ROUND 4 – BRISTOL 7 EXETER CHIEFS 35

(Sunday, February 5, Ashton Gate)

Bristol: L Arscott (S Piutau 19); J Williams (M Crumpton 34-43), J Tovey, B Mosses, C Amesbury (J Newey 62); C Sheedy, A Uren (M Roberts 66); J Ford-Robinson (T Rowland 74), M Jones (capt), J Hall (A Cleary 61); J Joyce (S Jeffries 22), I Evans; J Phillips, N Koster, J Crane (J Hawkins 61).

Chiefs: M Bodilly; O Woodburn, I Whitten (W Hooley 71), H Slade (M Jess 60), L Turner; J Simmonds, J Maunder (J Snow 66); C Rimmer (M Low 62), S Malton (J Innard 66), G Holmes (H Williams 47); S Skinner (capt), D Welch; B White (T Waldrom 60), J Salvi (O Atkins 53), S Simmonds.

Bristol: Try – Ford-Robinson; Conversion – Sheedy.
Chiefs: Tries – Malton, penalty tries (2), Slade, Bodilly; Conversions – J Simmonds (5).

Yellow Cards: Bristol – Jones, Phillips; Chiefs – Woodburn.

HT: 0-14. **Referee:** Ian Davies (Wales). **Attendance:** 8,875.

Exeter's Michele Campagnaro hands off Ulster's Ireland international fly-half Paddy Jackson

Referee Greg Garner pulls out the red card from his pocket to send off Jonny Hill after his high tackle on Wasps' Ashley Johnson

CHAPTER 7

Those Pesky Wasps

PREMIERSHIP TABLE							
	P	W	D	L	F	A	Pts
Wasps	17	13	1	3	537	371	64
EXETER	**17**	**10**	**3**	**4**	**490**	**335**	**59**
Saracens	17	12	1	4	417	247	58
Bath	17	10	0	7	362	294	48
Leicester	17	10	0	7	411	343	47
Northampton	17	9	0	8	356	339	44
Harlequins	17	9	0	8	382	395	42
Newcastle	17	7	0	10	339	443	36
Gloucester	17	5	2	10	408	399	35
Sale	17	5	1	11	335	435	29
Worcester	17	4	2	11	345	523	24
Bristol	17	3	0	14	277	535	17

FEBRUARY

Sunday 12	AP	D	Exeter Chiefs 35	Wasps 35
Saturday 18	AP	W	Worcester Warriors 32	Exeter Chiefs 48
Saturday 25	AP	W	Exeter Chiefs 36	Newcastle Falcons 14

MARCH

Friday 3	AP	W	Leicester Tigers 15	Exeter Chiefs 34

Premiership points available 20 – points taken 18

EXETER Chiefs went into the next block of Premiership fixtures sitting pretty in third place in the Premiership table.

They had an eight-point gap over fifth-spot Leicester, trailed second-position Saracens by seven, and were a further three behind leaders Wasps, who arrived at Sandy Park off the back of five straight league wins.

However, they had lost all nine of their previous visits to the Devon venue in all competitions, managing only two losing bonus points in the process.

'Dull' is just not in the vocabulary describing any matches between Exeter and Wasps, with their 2015-16 Champions Cup quarter-final at the Ricoh Arena, which the hosts won 25-24, still regarded by many seasoned old hacks as one of the best club games they have ever seen.

You could trot out several other examples of wonderful clashes involving the two rivals, so there was a huge air of expectancy going into this top-three battle, and the hype was fully justified as spectators were in for another treat.

With the Premiership's top two try scorers battling it out, with Wasps on 51 and Exeter on 41, well ahead of next-best Gloucester with 35, it was never going to be a kick fest, but five converted tries apiece in a 35-35 draw was something a bit special.

If it had been a Twickenham final, the two sides were so closely matched that it would have gone to extra time….. oh hang on, we are three months too early here!

Exeter had learned some valuable lessons from watching Saracens playing with only 14 men for 69 minutes of their game against the Chiefs five weeks before.

They now had the chance to put those into practice after a red card for former Gloucester Academy second row Jonny Hill early in the second half, for what was deemed by referee Greg Garner to be a high hit to the head of Wasps skipper Ashley Johnson.

It was the correct decision by the letter of the new tackle directives introduced during the campaign, though it was clumsy rather than anything malicious.

It was 28-21 to Exeter at the time of the unfortunate incident in a game, played in cold and blustery conditions, that had see-sawed this way and that in front of a crowd of over 12,000 people.

Baxter had sprung a surprise in his selection for the game by giving a first Premiership start to Sam Simmonds at No.8, with Thomas Waldrom nowhere to be seen in the match-day 23.

Luke Cowan-Dickie wriggles over for a try, despite the best efforts of Wasps scrum-half Dan Robson

A special moment for young scrum-half Jack Maunder as he scores his first Premiership try, against Wasps

It was a fitting reward for Simmonds, who had started the season dual-registered with Championship side Cornish Pirates, after two excellent Anglo-Welsh Cup performances, and he had just signed a new two-year deal with the club.

Wasps were missing the likes of Elliot Daly, Joe Launchbury, James Haskell, Nathan Hughes and Matt Mullan to RBS Six Nations duty with England, but Chiefs themselves were without Jack Nowell, Tomas Francis and Michele Campagnaro due to their own international call-ups.

Three times Wasps led in the first half, only to be pegged back on each occasion in a match where the respective kickers, Gareth Steenson and Jimmy Gopperth, both had immaculate five-from-five returns, despite the blustery conditions.

First-half tries by Christian Wade, a penalty try and Alex Rieder for Wasps were cancelled out by touchdowns from Simmonds, Jack Maunder for his first Premiership try after a great break by Phil Dollman, and another penalty try for collapsing a maul, to make it 21-21 at the break.

A Luke Cowan-Dickie touchdown early in the second half, after he had picked a lovely line off Steenson's pass, put Exeter ahead for the first time, but that was swiftly followed by Hill's red card, and a converted score a minute later by Kyle Eastmond after Danny Cipriani's beautifully-delayed pass left it all square.

Despite their one-man disadvantage, Olly Woodburn manage to wriggle his way over for Exeter before being replaced by Sam Skinner, as the Chiefs opted for an eight-man pack.

They pounded away at the Wasps line, but they were kept out, and when Exeter kicked away possession with 10 minutes remaining, Wasps countered with deadly effect, with replacement scrum-half Joe Simpson finishing off in style after former New Zealand All Blacks winger Frank Halai had made good ground, and Gopperth converted to leave it honours even.

Wasps director of rugby Dai Young gave his usual very fair assessment of the game.

"There was lots of good stuff from us, we had opportunities which we didn't take, but I am pretty pleased with three points at Exeter. It is a game we could have won, but we could easily have lost it as well, and it was a great game of rugby for the neutrals to watch," he said.

"The sending off was unfortunate. I don't think for one minute there was any malice in it, and it was just a mistimed clear-out, but the directives are what they are."

Baxter felt it was a match where the Chiefs learnt several good lessons which would hold them in good stead come the season's dramatic finale.

"We were becoming a confident team, we had won some important games, and we knew we were playing pretty well. There was a strong wind that day, we won the toss and chose to play into it first, and I genuinely think we thought it was okay to just kind of manage the early part of that game, and if we did that we would be able to come out on top of Wasps because we were fit and strong, and nobody else in the Premiership could challenge our ball-in-play time," he explained.

"That is ultimately a large part of what we decided to do as a team – to challenge everybody on work rate, by keeping the ball on the pitch and keeping the ball-in-play time very high.

"When you watch the beginning of that game and how easily we conceded points in that first half, it was a little bit scary.

"It was almost like our attitude was that it was okay to concede some soft scores in the first half because it would be alright in the second half, and we very nearly lost that game by not having the right intensity level right at the start of the game.

"The lesson we learned that day was 'if you want to challenge a team on work rate, it is no good thinking you will come through at the end if you don't challenge them right from minute one'.

"The frustrating thing from our perspective was that, just as it felt like we had turned the corner and were getting on top of them, having taken the lead early in the second half with a try and now having the elements in our favour, we had Jonny Hill sent off.

"It was another good lesson learnt by us because we didn't react quickly enough to that from either a coaching or team perspective, because almost immediately the ball was in our corner and they walked in a try and it was easy for them.

"We probably could have reacted a bit quicker sat in the grandstand and said: 'It is a day where we need eight forwards on the field'.

"We then re-adjusted and got a full pack of forwards on there by sacrificing a back.

"We then learnt another good lesson because we ended up losing the game based on kicking the ball away with a relatively short amount of time left, when we had been controlling possession.

"We drove a maul up the far side, we kicked them the ball, they managed to get it into the open, and all of a sudden they were scoring a breakaway try, which meant the game was a draw, after we had scored points with 14 men and done pretty much everything right.

Hooker Shaun Malton leading the post-match song in the Twickenham dressing room after beating Wasps in the Premiership final. It was a regular event during the Chiefs' season and endeared him to the players and coaches

"They were nice lessons for us to learn, that became very important by the end of the season."

Remember the closing stages of the Twickenham final, when Exeter turned down a kickable penalty and possible drop-goal attempts, just to hang on to possession and deny Wasps any ball.

"It was nice that we kept learning throughout the season, and we managed to do that while at the same time not losing, which in the shake-up was very important," added Baxter.

It was just after the Wasps game that Exeter signed experienced 30-year-old Bristol scrum-half Martin Roberts, who had also played in the Premiership for Northampton and Bath, with Will Chudley, Dave Lewis and Niko Matawalu all out injured.

But the fact that he never made a first-team appearance between then and the end of the season was down to the way youngsters Maunder – who was named in the England squad for the summer to tour Argentina – and Stuart Townsend handled their sudden promotion into the first team.

"We did expect a lot from them, and to be fair to them they stepped up," said Baxter.

"They didn't get everything perfect, and that Wasps game was perhaps an example of that, where we thought we had got a message on to Stu about how we wanted to play off that line-out where we conceded that late try.

"There was a bit of a jumble-up in the message, and the ball got kicked away, but all of those are things they have been able to learn from and adapt to.

"The truth is, a bit like with the development of Olly Woodburn, they needed time on the field, and as long as they are good guys and they work hard and they take the message on board, that's how they are going to get better.

"You can't criticise them in the attitude they have shown, in how hard they have worked and wanted to learn, and how quickly they have recovered when they have been injured, and the two of them were a key factor for us over the course of the season."

Six days later, the Chiefs headed to Sixways to play a Worcester side who posed a danger to Exeter as they were fresh from a 24-18 home win over defending champions Saracens.

They had won three of their last four games in all competitions but were still only five points clear of bottom club Bristol.

The Chiefs were hoping to avoid becoming the first side in Premiership history to draw three successive league games.

It is a match that I will always refer to as the 'Shaun Malton game' because the South African-born hooker, who had celebrated his 27th birthday three days before, was given an 11th hour call-up to the starting XV after club captain Jack Yeandle had been sick in the changing room just before kick-off, with Luke Cowan-Dickie already ruled out with a knee problem.

It was his first Premiership start since joining the club from Championship side Nottingham 20 months before, after a campaign in which he had been named the Midlanders' Player of the Season, but he produced his best ever display in an Exeter shirt, which ultimately saw him rewarded with a new contract for the 2017-18 season.

"We were hoping Yenz was going to come through. He had been suffering from a bit of sickness, but our thoughts going into the game were that 'we know he is not very well, but if he comes through the warm-up and he can go okay for 20 minutes or half an hour, then that will probably be enough for us'," explained Baxter.

Gareth Steenson flops over for a pretty rare try for the Chiefs - this one at Sixways

"Yenz did the warm-up, Shaun wasn't expected to start and was ready to relax and sit on the bench, and I remember giving him a tap and saying 'you're starting', and he looked at me a bit panicked but I told him he would be fine.

"He had a fantastic match and it really was the 'Shaun Malton game'.

"The face of Elvis Taione (who was just coming back from a broken thumb) was a picture as well when I told him he was on the bench, because I think he'd had quite a nice breakfast! And he stepped up as well.

"It is those kinds of moments that make seasons, and we had those moments where guys had to step in and perform for us, and to a man, where we had injuries or little things happened, they did fantastically well.

"I was really pleased for Shaun how well it went, and it gave him that opportunity to knock himself up a notch or two in the coaches' eyes and the team's eyes."

Baxter added: "Shaun is one of those background stories of the season. He got himself involved in the match-day 23, but he also took on leading the post-match song in the dressing room (not really suitable for family listening!).

"I am not going to tell you what it is about or say the words, but you see him strutting around in the middle, and the guys really like it, and during the course of the season it kind of became their celebration song.

"It would happen on a Saturday, and sometimes they would do it in training on a Monday, if they felt like it, and to be fair, Shaun is one of those guys who found a niche for himself within the squad, largely based on training well and performing well and showing some character, and although he wasn't actually involved on the field in the final, he was involved in the post-match celebrations, and he was a driver and an important part of the qualities we showed over the season."

After the previous week's 10 tries in the match against Wasps, Chiefs fans had another 11 to savour against Worcester – seven of them to Exeter, with James Short helping himself to a hat-trick to take him to 10 for the season – eight in the Premiership.

Exeter were proving to be one of the hottest tickets in town, with an incredible 55 tries being scored in the last six games they had been involved in, with Chiefs getting 34 of them.

But it was a match that arguably could have gone either way until, with the Warriors leading 18-17 early in the second half, Samoan international and former Bath No.8 Alafoti Faosiliva was yellow-carded for a rather brainless late shoulder charge on Don Armand, which proved very costly for Worcester, as they conceded 19 points while he was off the field.

The Warriors, full of confidence after downing Sarries, flew out of the blocks with two tries inside the first 14 minutes.

Young full-back Josh Adams got the first after four minutes, and winger Perry Humphreys the second after they had created an overlap.

James Short slides in for one of his hat-trick of tries against Worcester on another 'hot' day for the winger

Fly-half Ryan Mills, the kicking hero against Sarries, converted one and added a penalty, while Exeter replied in between the two home touchdowns with a try by skipper Steenson, who sold a dummy to run in from 25 metres and he converted the score himself, to leave the Chiefs trailing 15-7.

Short finished off a move in the left-hand corner, improved by Steenson, to put the Chiefs right back in it, but after Mills had missed two more penalty chances, he slotted one, before Steenson replied on the stroke of half-time with his own successful kick to leave Exeter one point adrift at the break.

After Faosiliva's unnecessary misdemeanour, Woodburn dotted down in the corner; Short cut inside off his wing for his second after a great counter attack by Sam Simmonds and Dave Dennis; and Simmonds scored his second try in two games off a well-orchestrated driving maul, with centre Henry Slade converting two of them after Steenson had gone off with a hamstring problem.

Exeter suddenly led 36-18 and the match had a totally different complexion, but Worcester stuck to their task well after being restored to their full complement.

Kiwi winger Bryce Heem dotted down beneath the uprights after an initial try-saving tackle by Slade on Jackson Willison, with Mills converting, but Exeter's reply was instant, with Italian international Michele Campagnaro making it seven tries in his last four games for Exeter, with Slade improving the score.

With six minutes remaining, Short completed his hat-trick after taking a wonderful pass from Slade and turning on the after-burners, but there was still time for Worcester to score a crucial bonus-point fourth try with the last play of the game, through Willison, converted by replacement Ryan Lamb, which put them six points clear of Bristol, who were hammered at Leicester.

Sam Simmonds shows his delight at finishing off some hard work by his fellow forwards at Worcester

"We highlighted some key areas where we really felt we could go after Worcester," explained Baxter.

"I actually felt okay with the way Worcester started that game, even though they scored two early tries, because they looked like they were out on their feet scoring their second try.

"I remember saying to Ali and Rob, 'that score has hurt them', and we made them work really hard to get their points on the board.

"They were the perfect example where we could say 'if we keep this game playing and keep this ball moving, and keep going and going, can you stand with us?, and they might be one of those teams we can really challenge'.

"They were having to hurt themselves to score points against us, and although you obviously don't want to concede points, the process of us coming through that game was there, and we eventually got on top and we pulled away.

"We showed some really, really top qualities that day, and it sounds very simple but they were largely based around hard work and individuals driving themselves through some pretty tough situations."

Short's contribution was another example of how much he seemed to love scoring tries away from home, with 11 of his 14 touchdowns during the campaign coming on the club's travels, and it was form that saw him win the Premiership Player of the Month award for February.

"His stats for the amount of tries he scored away from home for us were phenomenal and he has got some fantastic qualities," said Baxter.

"He was a little frustrated with his season seeing him in and out of the starting line-up, but he should be frustrated and it should be a huge driver for him.

"He has always trained really well and come in and been very diligent and ready to go, and he was lethal for us in some very important games."

Short carried on his hot streak with two more tries – one in each half – in a comfortable 36-14 home victory over Newcastle Falcons.

There was also a very assured performance on his first Premiership start for 20-year-old fly-half Joe Simmonds as he replaced the injured Steenson, who was joined on the treatment table by Australian Dave Dennis after he also injured a hamstring in the captain's run the day before the game.

Backs coach Ali Hepher praised Simmonds after the match, saying: "I am pleased for Joe. He steps in for Steeno and there are no dramas. You don't have to talk to him to build his confidence or anything like that. He is steady and rock solid, and we have been really pleased with him ever since he has been at the club.

"Every little step he has had to take to the next level, he has taken in his stride, and he just keeps things very simple for himself."

It was a victory that moved the Chiefs into second place in the Premiership table – where they would stay over the remaining six weeks of the regular league season – one point clear of Saracens and six behind leaders Wasps.

James Short goes for a gap between Newcastle duo Will Welch and Vereniki Goneva on his way to one of the tries of the season at Sandy Park

The Falcons had never won at Sandy Park before but led 14-7 with more than half an hour played – and that was to become a recurring theme for the Chiefs over three successive home games against teams in the bottom half of the table.

Baxter has always joked down through the years that the Chiefs never believe in doing things the easy way, and the fixtures against the Falcons, Sale Sharks and Bristol proved that once again.

However, Exeter got their noses in front before half-time and controlled the second half to pick up the bonus-point win which moved them ahead of Sarries, who managed a three-try 29-18 victory over Sale Sharks.

Flying Fijian winger Vereniki Goneva scored a try in the corner for Newcastle after only four minutes, converted from the touchline by Tongan scrum-half Sonatane Takulua, but then came an incident ten minutes later that Hepher admitted had been a crucial moment in the contest.

Goneva intercepted a pass by Waldrom – restored to the starting line-up – and broke clear downfield and was only stopped from scoring a second try by a tackle from Dollman, who had a fine game. When possession was recycled, full-back Alex Tait had the line at his mercy, only to spill the ball, and from the knock-on, Short raced 90 metres to touch down beneath the posts, with Joe Simmonds kicking the simple conversion, making it 7-7, instead of 14-0 to a Newcastle side enjoying their best Premiership campaign in years and fresh from an impressive home win over Northampton.

The Falcons did manage a second try, through prop Rob Vickers after an initial break by back rower Callum Chick, improved by Takulua, to make it 14-7 after 23 minutes, but they surprisingly never scored again in the match.

A first Premiership try for Exeter by tight-head prop Harry Williams, converted by Simmonds, who added a penalty, gave the Chiefs what at one point had seemed an unlikely 17-14 half-time lead, and with the wind behind them in the second half, they took control.

A penalty try from a scrum, followed by a first Premiership try for replacement Sam Skinner only a minute after coming on, after a howler on his own line by former New Zealand All Blacks fly-half Mike Delany, with both scores improved by Simmonds, put the Chiefs out of sight, and a clever grubber kick through by replacement stand-off Will Hooley for Short's second of the game was the icing on the cake.

The Chiefs completed this block of Premiership fixtures with a Friday night trip to Leicester, hoping to complete a league double over the Tigers.

Beating them convincingly at Sandy Park on Christmas Eve was one thing. Defeating them at Welford Road would be another kettle of fish, especially as the Tigers had Premiership semi-final aspirations of their own, lying one point outside the top four.

Sam Skinner scores his first Premiership try, going over beneath the posts against Newcastle

Exeter had not won there in the league since 2011, but they did lower the Tigers' colours on their own patch in an Anglo-Welsh Cup semi-final in 2015, and this was to be an excellent indicator of how serious their hopes of winning the Premiership title were.

The Chiefs gave a first Premiership start to Townsend, with Slade back from England duty at fly-half and Armand captaining a side which included former Tigers favourites Geoff Parling and Waldrom.

If Worcester was the 'Shaun Malton game', this will go down as the 'Geoff Parling game' as he produced an immense, man-of-the-match display – something which, quite frankly, Exeter fans had not seen too many of from the former England and British and Irish Lion lock in his first 18 months at the club.

Even though he had been quietly efficient in his performances, he had never stood out for me in the way I thought he would when he made the move to Sandy Park in the summer of 2015.

I also broke a story at this time that he had failed to agree terms on a new deal with the Chiefs, and was in talks with Super Rugby side Melbourne Rebels, who he subsequently joined at the end of the season.

However, whatever your views on his first year-and-a-half at the club, no-one could deny that he was magnificent in the last four months of the season and played a major part in Exeter winning the Premiership.

Baxter defended the player against any criticism, and commented: "I think Geoff has been very important for us, and I think he was important the season before as well, and guys add more to the squad than just what you see on the field.

"I think Geoff was almost what you would describe as a bit of a 'big game player', he had his best games in big, important matches for us, and I think you started to see that as the season wore on.

"Every game in the final few months of the season was probably going to decide what was going to happen in the top four, and I think that really suited him, and it really brought the best out of him.

"It probably also suited him knowing that he was likely to be involved in the team, because we had limited numbers (Mitch Lees, Jonny Hill and Dave Dennis were all injured at different times), and the pressure that was going to be put on him was that he had to play well because there wasn't going to be the opportunity to have a week off or have a bit of a break.

"It was: 'I am going to have to be bang on here, and if I want to drive this team to win the final and be part of it, I am going to have to play well'.

"He is a good character so he thrived under that real leadership and involvement, and getting ready to play week by week."

Interestingly, speaking after the match, the 33-year-old Parling described the win over Leicester as one of the biggest of his career, which is some statement coming from a man who had won 54 England caps, played for the Lions three times, and captured the Premiership title with Leicester in 2010 and 2013.

"To win at Leicester is a huge statement for us," he said. "We have been on a bit of a roll lately and not only have we been winning games, we've been picking up bonus points. To come away to the Tigers – and I know what playing at Welford Road means to Leicester players – I thought we turned up and did a fantastic job. I think tonight we showed we are a good team, so let's make these games count for something. Let's go and finish in that top two.

"Last year was a good season and we got to the final, but it wasn't a really successful season. It was a statement for the club, but an even bigger statement is to go on and win the Premiership." He added: "I was trying to get the message across last year that we shouldn't be happy with losing. I don't think we were, but look at Saracens before they started to win everything. They lost a few finals and you do learn from them. If that's your first experience of a final, you do learn from those experiences and let's make sure we have learnt from them." Prophetic words from the big man, and if anyone had any doubts before the Leicester game that Exeter could win the title, they were firmly assuaged by the Welford Road display. Leicester, who went into the game seeking their fourth straight Premiership win for the first time in two years, just had no answer to a Chiefs side who stretched their unbeaten league run to 10 games.

I felt at the time it was their best Premiership performance of the season, but they had to come through some worrying early moments.

Baxter had been looking for a fast start from his troops, but it was Leicester's Italian international prop Michele Rizzo who scored a fourth-minute try from close range, despite more than a suspicion of a double movement.

No way through for Phil Dollman at Leicester as he is tackled by Tom Youngs and Telusa Veainu

However, the Chiefs struck back only three minutes later when openside flanker Kai Horstmann celebrated his new one-year contract by charging down Leicester fly-half Owen Williams' attempted clearance kick to score beneath the posts to give stand-off Slade the easiest of conversions.

The Chiefs then produced an amazing 25-phase defensive set to keep Tigers out, though they did finally cough up a penalty, which Williams slotted, to edge Tigers 8-7 in front, but Slade responded with a penalty of his own to make it 10-8 to the visitors, and the Chiefs were never headed again in the match.

Exeter's 10th penalty try of the season, for Tigers collapsing a maul heading for their line and which saw England hooker Tom Youngs sin-binned, converted by Slade, stretched the advantage.

Townsend then grabbed his first Premiership try, sneaking over in the corner after Parling had almost made it to the whitewash himself following a looping pass by Slade, who masterfully converted from the touchline, adding a penalty in first-half injury time, and Exeter led 27-8 at the break.

The expected Tigers onslaught materialised at the start of the second period as French international centre Maxime Mermoz squirmed over beside the posts, and Williams converted.

Winger Adam Thompstone also had a possible try ruled out by television match official Graham Hughes after his knee broke the whitewash as he touched down, and even after losing Parling to a yellow card for repeated infringement by the Chiefs, Lees drove over for the bonus-point fourth try, converted by Slade, to seal a famous victory.

With the likes of Jack Nowell, Campagnaro, Steenson, Will Chudley and Dave Ewers to add back into the squad, it was an exciting time for Exeter.

"We produced our best performance of the season in parts of that game," admitted Baxter. "Defensively, our work in the contact area was absolutely fantastic. When we do a defensive review, we show the top tackles and the best moments defensively from games, and I remember there being so many from that match. I remember Ollie Devoto, in particular, not just stopping Leicester players but literally carrying them back up the field.

"You look at the set-piece pressure we started to exert, and the important set-piece moments we survived and came away on top from. Like many games in the season, it also showed how the 23 players, over the course of 80 minutes, could really come together. Stu Townsend was fantastic that day. He kicked exceptionally well, he was very good defensively and he scored an important try for us, and that was a game where a young man really showed some fantastic qualities. In a lot of ways, that was probably one of the most satisfying performances of our season." Former Leicester fly-half Bleddyn Jones, who commentates for *BBC Radio Leicester*, paid Exeter Chiefs the ultimate compliment after the game.

"It was like watching Tigers in their pomp," he told me, no doubt referring to the great Leicester side of the early 2000s that mopped up seven Premiership titles and two Heineken Cups in the space of 11 years.

Exeter players celebrate their fantastic win over Leicester at Welford Road

PREMIERSHIP

ROUND 14 – EXETER CHIEFS 35 WASPS 35

(Sunday, February 12, Sandy Park)

Chiefs: P Dollman; O Woodburn (S Skinner 52), I Whitten, O Devoto (H Slade 74), J Short; G Steenson (capt), J Maunder (S Townsend 66); B Moon (C Rimmer 54), L Cowan-Dickie (J Yeandle 64), G Holmes (H Williams 48); M Lees, J Hill; D Dennis (T Johnson 65), D Armand, S Simmonds. Replacement (not used): L Turner.

Wasps: K Beale; C Wade, J Gopperth, K Eastmond (A Leiua 71), J Bassett (F Halai 65); D Cipriani, D Robson (J Simpson 65); S McIntyre, C Festuccia (J Gaskell 52), M Moore (J Cooper-Woolley 55); M Symons, K Myall (W Rowlands 52); A Johnson (capt), T Young, A Rieder. Replacements (not used): T Cruse, T Bristow.

Chiefs: Tries – S Simmonds, Maunder, penalty try, Cowan-Dickie, Woodburn; Conversions – Steenson (5).
Wasps: Tries – Wade, penalty try, Rieder, Eastmond, Simpson; Conversions – Gopperth (5).

Red Card: Chiefs – J Hill. **Yellow Cards:** Chiefs – Lees; Wasps – Young.

HT: 21-21. **Referee:** Greg Garner (RFU). **Attendance:** 12,036.

ROUND 15 –

WORCESTER WARRIORS 32 EXETER CHIEFS 48

(Saturday, February 18, Sixways Stadium)

Worcester: J Adams; B Heem, W Olivier, J Willison, P Humphreys (B Howard 61); R Mills (R Lamb 67), F Hougaard (L Baldwin 64); R Bower (N Leleimalefaga 55), J Bregvadze (J Taufete'e 55), N Schonert (B Alo 69); D O' Callaghan (capt) (T Cavubati 61), W Spencer; C Vui, D Potgieter (S Lewis 64), A Faosiliva.

Chiefs: P Dollman (L Turner 69); O Woodburn, M Campagnaro, H Slade, J Short; G Steenson (capt) (I Whitten 49), J Maunder (S Townsend 65); B Moon (C Rimmer 53), S Malton (E Taione 74), H Williams (T Francis 53); M Lees, G Parling; D Dennis (S Skinner 69) D Armand, S Simmonds (T Waldrom 55).

Worcester: Tries – Adams, Humphreys, Heem, Willison; Conversions – Mills (2), Lamb; Penalties – Mills (2).
Chiefs: Tries – Steenson, Short (3), Woodburn, S Simmonds, Campagnaro; Conversions – Steenson (2), Slade (3); Penalty – Steenson.

Yellow Card: Worcester – Faosiliva.

HT: 18-17. **Referee:** JP Doyle (RFU). **Attendance:** 8,738.

ROUND 16

EXETER CHIEFS 36 NEWCASTLE FALCONS 14

(Saturday, February 25, Sandy Park)

Chiefs: P Dollman; O Woodburn, I Whitten, O Devoto (S Hill 57), J Short; J Simmonds (W Hooley 74), J Maunder (S Townsend 57); B Moon (C Rimmer 61), J Yeandle (capt, S Malton 72), H Williams (M Low 74); M Lees (O Atkins 75), G Parling; K Horstmann (S Skinner 72), D Armand, T Waldrom.

Newcastle: A Tait, V Goneva, C Harris, D Waldouck (F Burdon 70), S Sinoti; J Hodgson (M Delany 57), S Takulua (S Egerton 70); R Vickers (B Harris 57), B Sowrey (S Lawson 57), S Wilson (D Wilson ht); C Green, E Olmstead (G Young 70); C Chick, W Welch (capt), N Latu (A Hogg 64).

Chiefs: Tries – Short (2), Williams, penalty try, Skinner; Conversions – J Simmonds (4); Penalty – J Simmonds.
Newcastle: Tries – Goneva, Vickers; Conversions – Takulua (2).

HT: 17-14. **Referee:** Ian Tempest (RFU). **Attendance:** 10,469.

ROUND 17 – LEICESTER TIGERS 15 EXETER CHIEFS 34

(Friday, March 3, Welford Road)

Leicester: T Veainu; A Thompstone, M Smith (F Burns 56), M Mermoz, JP Pietersen (G McGuigan 27-37); O Williams; J Kitto (S Harrison 46, P Betham 58); M Rizzo (E Genge ht), T Youngs (capt) (G McGuigan 55), G Bateman (P Cilliers 55); M Fitzgerald, D Barrow; T Croft (M Williams 46), B O'Connor, L Hamilton (L McCaffrey 74).

Chiefs: P Dollman; O Woodburn, I Whitten, O Devoto, J Short (S Hill 70); H Slade (J Simmonds 79), S Townsend (J Maunder 60); C Rimmer (B Moon 49), L Cowan-Dickie (J Yeandle 60), H Williams (T Francis 49); M Lees (S Simmonds 70), G Parling (J Hill 64); D Armand (capt), K Horstmann, T Waldrom.

Leicester: Tries – Rizzo, Mermoz; Conversion – O Williams; Penalty – O Williams.
Chiefs: Tries – Horstmann, penalty try, Townsend, Lees; Conversions – Slade (4); Penalties – Slade (2).

Yellow Cards: Leicester – T Youngs; Chiefs – Parling.

HT: 8-27. **Referee:** Matt Carley (RFU). **Attendance:** 20,434.

Dave Ewers drives Exeter forward in an excellent performance against Harlequins on his first Premiership start of the season

Exeter Chiefs

CHAPTER 8

Trouble At Mill

PREMIERSHIP TABLE							
	P	W	D	L	F	A	Pts
Wasps	20	16	1	3	645	455	79
EXETER	**20**	**13**	**3**	**4**	**597**	**420**	**74**
Saracens	20	15	1	4	537	301	72
Leicester	20	12	0	8	498	404	57
Bath	20	11	0	9	418	393	53
Northampton	20	9	0	11	442	434	48
Harlequins	20	10	0	10	480	491	47
Gloucester	20	7	2	11	493	459	46
Newcastle	20	8	0	12	375	540	40
Sale	20	6	1	13	426	530	36
Worcester	20	5	2	13	429	618	31
Bristol	20	3	0	17	346	641	19

MARCH

Sunday 12	AWC	W	Exeter Chiefs 24	Harlequins 7 (semi-final)
Sunday 19	AWC	L	Exeter Chiefs 12	Leicester Tigers 16 (final at Twickenham Stoop)
Saturday 25	AP	W	Exeter Chiefs 30	Sale Sharks 25

APRIL

Saturday 8	AP	W	Exeter Chiefs 38	Bristol 34
Friday 14	AP	W	Harlequins 26	Exeter Chiefs 39

Premiership points available 15 – points taken 15

THE penultimate block of fixtures in the regular Premiership season need to be viewed against the backdrop of Exeter's involvement in the latter stages of the Anglo-Welsh Cup.

The fall-out from the final at the Twickenham Stoop – ironically just across the road from the stadium where they would so gloriously triumph two-and-a-half months later – almost derailed the Chiefs' title ambitions.

The fact that did not happen is down to the players realising they were in danger of throwing away the whole season, and for taking on board what they were being told by the Rob Baxter and his coaching staff.

Baxter took the unusual decision, straight after the Leicester game, of resting pretty much all of his frontline players for the next three weeks, bar those that were needed as injury cover.

I say unusual because, whenever Exeter had faced two-match Anglo-Welsh Cup blocks in past seasons, he had tended to go for more of a mix-and-match approach, giving at least some of his first-team players a run-out in the second game to keep them match sharp ahead of the return to Premiership action.

Only three players who had started against the Tigers kicked off the home semi-final with Harlequins at Sandy Park nine days later – Ollie Devoto, Stuart Townsend and Harry Williams, and only two – James Short and Carl Rimmer – the final against Leicester.

Baxter was looking at the bigger picture, thinking ahead to the tough league matches that still lay ahead for the Chiefs, and a potential semi-final and final, and the management of his squad at this stage ultimately proved crucial in the final analysis.

You could see the physical benefits of that decision he took in early March in the extra-time period at Twickenham, when the players' fitness levels were incredible, and they were able to keep bashing away against a visibly tiring Wasps side.

"You are always hoping that the season is going to keep going for you, and at some stage you have got to make those calls, and we did it then, and in hindsight it was important for us," explained Baxter.

"It is always a tough one regarding how you will come through it, and probably the only judge ever is hindsight.

"As we look back now, it was a really good call, but could it have backfired on us? Well, maybe, but it did feel like we had a group of players who were putting in a lot of intensity, and it is not just the intensity they are putting into playing, it is the intensity they are driving through training as well.

"I think we had also asked a lot of the guys emotionally, and for a lot of them it was just good to get away from each other and have a bit of an emotional break from saying: 'What is the next game going to bring?', because sometimes, you need a mental freshen up as much as you need a physical one."

Top: Max Bodilly races towards the line to score a try in the Anglo-Welsh Cup semi-final against Harlequins

Middle: Lachie Turner cuts the Harlequins defence to ribbons to get a touchdown in the Anglo-Welsh Cup semi-final at Sandy Park

Bottom right: Jonny Hill (left) and Elvis Taione celebrate Sam Simmonds' match-clinching try to book their place in the Anglo-Welsh Cup final

Bottom left: Sam Simmonds' late try at the Twickenham Stoop gives Exeter hope of denying Leicester the Anglo-Welsh Cup

You could argue, and many would, that Baxter sacrificed the chance to pick up one piece of silverware – a cup that Exeter had won in 2014 – in the hope of landing the bigger prize, though he was still optimistic he had selected a side for the Anglo-Welsh Cup semi-final and final that could go on and win the competition, but Baxter feels that assessment is too simplistic.

"When you look at the team that Leicester played in the final, compared to our line-up, you can obviously see a load more what you would call frontline players, but I think we will really benefit, and did benefit, from some of those lads playing in that game," explained Baxter.

"For Jack Maunder and Joe Simmonds at half-back, it was absolutely fantastic for them, and we also kept some other players topped up with game time, which was very important – guys who would get bench spots or be rotated in over the closing weeks of the season, which was also hugely important for us, and at the end of the day, we didn't lose the final by that much."

Despite making 12 changes to the starting line-up from the Leicester game, the semi-final against Harlequins at Sandy Park ended up being a pretty routine win, with the Chiefs producing a dominant display from start to finish to triumph 24-7, courtesy of tries from Lachie Turner after a sublime, mazy 30-metre run; Max Bodilly following some fancy footwork; Julian Salvi for his first try of the season; and Sam Simmonds from a catch-and-drive line-out move, with his younger brother Joe slotting two conversions.

What was not routine was the spectacular delivery of the match ball before kick-off, on a zip-wire across the pitch, by the Royal Marine Commandos.

It was a nightmare for Quins, who named a pretty powerful side but ended up not making a final that was being played at their home ground seven days later. They would be hosting a party to which they had not been invited!

As a result, the final was sadly played in front of a crowd of only 6,834.

The Chiefs made five changes for their third successive Anglo-Welsh Cup final.

Leicester, meanwhile, repeated what they had done for the semi-final against Saracens, by naming a strong line-up that included the likes of Graham Kitchener, Freddie Burns, Lachie McCaffrey, Peter Betham and former Plymouth Albion loanee Ellis Genge.

I am sure, at that stage, the best the Tigers felt they could get out of what had been a somewhat indifferent Premiership campaign by their high standards was an away semi-final.

The Anglo-Welsh Cup offered them the chance to salvage something and secure a first trophy for the club in four long years – much-needed having lost the city's sporting limelight in recent times to near-neighbours Leicester City after they had incredibly won the Premier League title.

As a result, they went very strong with their selections for both the semi-final and final, despite having a big East Midlands derby away to Northampton Saints on their return to Premiership action, which would be crucial to their top-four hopes. Full credit to the Tigers, as they went on to win that game against their arch-rivals as well, 36-31.

Fourteen of their 23-man squad for the cup final had featured in their last Premiership game – that 34-15 home defeat to the Chiefs – whereas Exeter only included six who had played at Welford Road, and one of those was a late call-up, with Rimmer replacing the injured Moray Low.

Excellent Bath-bound fly-half Burns kicked Leicester into an early lead with a penalty, but Short continued his rich scoring vein with another fine try after a clever miss-move in midfield.

The Tigers claimed their first try of the game when Tom Brady intercepted a pass from Matt Jess to race in – interception tries were to become a worryingly recurring theme for the Chiefs over the coming weeks – and with Burns converting and adding two penalties, the Tigers led 16-5 at the break.

It was sadly not proving a good kicking day for young Joe Simmonds, as he missed a first-half conversion and a penalty, and another long-range penalty attempt early in the second period.

Exeter thought they had scored a try soon after through Maunder, but the touchdown was reviewed by the TMO, and a knock-on by Salvi earlier in the move was spotted.

The Chiefs kept battering away at the Tigers, and they went through an incredible 35-phase passage of play, but Leicester held firm.

However, they did finally manage to get across the whitewash with two minutes remaining, with Sam Simmonds powering under the sticks and replacement Will Hooley converting, but any prospect of a further score was ended by the clock and the game was lost 16-12.

It was a much happier day than two years before for Leicester's replacement hooker Greg Bateman.

Playing for Exeter, he had unfortunately given away the late penalty that saw former Ivybridge Community College student Ben Spencer slot the match-winning kick for Saracens in the 2015 LV= Cup final at Franklin's Gardens.

"I would much rather be on this side of the fence and the feeling is just brilliant," Bateman told *BBC Radio Devon* after defeating his former club.

It was the seventh time in eight one-match 'cup' finals (ignoring the two-legged Championship final) Exeter had lost – four National Trophy finals, two Anglo-Welsh Cup finals and a Premiership final.

Little did we know then what was just around the corner!

Little did Leicester head coach Aaron Mauger know what was just around the corner either. Having won the Tigers their first piece of silverware since 2013, and with the taste of champagne having barely left his lips, he was incredibly sacked the following day, to be replaced by Matt O'Connor.

Kai Horstmann notches his second try in two Premiership matches in the home game against Sale Sharks

Putting the cup final disappointment quickly behind them, the Chiefs headed into their next two Premiership games, and with no disrespect to Sale Sharks and Bristol, they were coming to Sandy Park with both of them lying in the bottom three in the table, and anything short of a 10-point haul for Exeter was going to be a major shock.

Leaders Wasps and third-place Saracens also had back-to-back home fixtures in this two-match period, but with Sarries having the toughest task with games against Bath and Harlequins at Allianz Park, it looked like an ideal chance for the Chiefs to take a huge step towards nailing down second position, and even putting pressure on Wasps at the top.

Chiefs made only two changes from the team that had won last time out in the league at Welford Road, with Jack Nowell (back from England Six Nations duty) and Ben Moon coming in for Short and Rimmer.

My big concern going into the Sale clash was how undercooked were the Chiefs' frontline players going to be after a three-week break without a game? Would they be refreshed or rusty?

The answer appeared to be 'rusty' as Exeter produced a strangely faltering, off-colour display but still managed a 30-25 bonus-point victory to once again extend their unbeaten run in the league to 11 matches.

Sale had a ferocious wind behind their backs in the first half, and American international fly-half AJ MacGinty, who had a good game, made full use of it with some excellent goalkicking, with the Chiefs uncharacteristically giving away three scrum penalties.

Don Armand crashes over beside the posts against Sale Sharks, with Carl Rimmer in support

Two early MacGinty kicks put Sale 6-0 in front, and they extended their advantage when Samoan winger and Rugby League convert Denny Solomona intercepted – yes, that word again – a pass and ran 80 metres to score his ninth Premiership try of the season, with MacGinty adding the extras.

Exeter responded with a good break by hooker Luke Cowan-Dickie, in front of watching England forwards coach Steve Borthwick, which created a try in the corner for evergreen back rower Kai Horstmann.

Two more MacGinty penalties gave Sale a handy 19-5 lead, but the Chiefs got a crucial try just before the interval, with Cowan-Dickie finishing off a catch-and-drive, and Slade converting.

It meant they only trailed by seven points after a pretty torrid opening 40 minutes, and it was not long into the second period that an Olly Woodburn try and Slade penalty had got the Chiefs in front for the first time in the match at 20-19. Sale nosed ahead again with another MacGinty penalty, and the Exeter fans were starting to get very nervous until skipper-for-the-day Don Armand found a hole in the Sharks' defence to score under the posts in the 67th minute.

Slade converted, and his penalty four minutes from time sealed victory, but a three-pointer by MacGinty with the last kick of the game, which gave him a seven-from-seven record, earned the Sharks deserved consolation for their efforts.

That match had been traumatic enough for the Chiefs supporters so used to seeing their team winning in recent months, but it paled into insignificance compared to what they had to go through a fortnight later against Bristol, who were on the verge of having their relegation confirmed, after only one season back in the top flight.

Geoff Parling scores his first try for Exeter, and a crucial one at that, in the tense victory over bottom side Bristol

Exeter were boosted by the return of key figures such as Dave Ewers, Gareth Steenson, Greg Holmes and Michele Campagnaro to their bench for a game that saw the 3pm kick-off delayed by 15 minutes by Premiership Rugby, after an accident on the M5 motorway close to Sandy Park had caused traffic chaos.

Bristol were late getting to the ground as a result, and some supporters never made it at all as they were still stuck in their own cars in queues as the game progressed, or on buses bringing them from the park and ride, and it provoked an angry and unfair backlash against the club for something over which they had no control.

It was an incredible contest in which the lead changed hands several times, and the Chiefs needed a try three minutes from time by Thomas Waldrom to not only save their own blushes and break Bristol's hearts, after they had picked up their first try bonus point of the season, but also confirm Exeter's place in the Premiership semi-finals.

Many were expecting an avalanche of points from the hosts, and a try after only 70 seconds by Woodburn after he finished off a break by Ian Whitten, merely confirmed that expectation, with Slade converting.

But Chiefs were soon bemoaning a catalogue of handling errors, loose play and wrong decision-making, and Bristol roared back with two interception tries from Will Hurrell and Jason Woodward in the space of nine minutes, and two conversions and a penalty by Gavin Henson suddenly put Bristol 17-7 ahead.

A third converted try, by the excellent Henson, to a Slade penalty, made it 24-10 to the visitors, and it looked like the unthinkable, from an Exeter's point of view, might happen.

However, as against Sale, a try just before the break, in fact first-half injury time – and a first for the club by Geoff Parling, converted superbly by Slade – kept them in it.

They also began the second half as they had started the first, with a converted try inside the first minute by Whitten to level the scores, and when Waldrom finished off a catch-and-drive in the 53rd minute, and Slade added the extras, Exeter led 31-24.

Bristol were fighting for their Premiership lives though, and they responded with a Henson penalty and his conversion of Mitch Eadie's touchdown, to lead by three points.

That looked like being sufficient to secure a famous victory, until Waldrom crashed over for his ninth Premiership try of the season to the relief of the vast majority of the 12,000-plus crowd.

His try double took him to 51 Premiership tries, and he became only the 18th player in the league's history to reach the half-century landmark.

It was also the last time he would score during the season, and he ended the campaign with the second highest number of tries for a forward in the competition's history. Only former Leicester Tigers and England flanker Neil Back had more with 59, which he reached in 128 matches.

Back and Waldrom were in a league of their own in that list, with the next highest try-scoring forwards being Pat Lam and Phil Dowson tied on 29, and the Exeter No.8 would have got even closer to Back's tally in the 2016-17 season if a number of tries he thought he had scored, or was about to score, were not given as penalty tries, much to his annoyance!

Bitterly disappointed Bristol captain Marc Jones was aggrieved with the display of referee Tom Foley, and said: "We felt we put enough into the game to win. We came down here with a plan, which we executed, and we can be proud of our efforts, but effort alone doesn't get you across the line.

"I would like to see the penalty count and that is probably the biggest disappointment for us."

Two banana skins narrowly avoided, 10 points in the bag, job done.

They say the sign of a good team is one that does not perform well and still wins, and that seemed to be very much the case against Sale and Bristol, but there was more to those displays than met the eye, with issues rumbling on behind the scenes that were never revealed at that time.

It all harped back to that Anglo-Welsh Cup period, but it just showed the tremendous unity there was amongst the players, and the strong culture that existed and made the Chiefs such a formidable proposition.

"The truth was, as a squad, I don't think they really liked a decision I made not to take the whole squad to the Anglo-Welsh Cup final, because I wanted the frontline players to focus on the Premiership," explained Baxter.

"The cup final was on a Sunday, we had a turnaround into a Saturday game, and I wanted the players to train flat out on the Monday, and up and down to Harlequins in a day is not particularly good preparation for that.

"They rebelled a little bit as a squad, they said: 'We're all in this together, we should do everything together', and it created not a great training week, which led to a little bit of a flat performance against a team that were really going to come at us.

"I wouldn't say it caused ill feeling, but maybe proved a little bit of a distraction that just took us a little bit of working through and probably wasn't needed at the time, when we should have been fully focused on playing Sale and Bristol.

> We had to work exceptionally hard for a large part of that game to make the win happen, and that ultimately cost us bodies, and that frustrated me

"Looking back on it, would I sacrifice half a day's training or a day's training to keep the squad together? Maybe, rather than telling the rest of the squad that your focus is the next Premiership game, and I would probably approach that situation differently now.

"The flip to that though was we showed the qualities during both of those games to come through and win, and once we came through them, they became quite positive things for us.

"I remember having a go at the lads, I think it was after the Bristol game, and saying: 'You have been so close to letting the season slip out of your hands that I am incredibly angry with you. Are you seriously, at this stage of the season, when we have achieved so much, going to let a team come to Sandy Park and take the season away from you?'

"It was good for me to get it off my chest, and it was probably good for the lads to re-examine the fact that control of our season was in our hands.

"Once you are in the top four, if you keep winning every game of rugby, you will stay in the top four, which means you get a semi-final, and then it is in your hands to reach the final.

"We spoke a lot like that, and those two games were matches where maybe we allowed a little bit of slackness or complacency to creep in, and we nearly let somebody take our destiny out of our hands, and that really frustrated me because I knew we were a better side than that.

"It was also nice to be able to top up and reassert the message we had talked about a few months earlier, that each game is in your hands, and what happens in the 80 minutes, you can drive it or you let the opposition drive it."

Despite the closeness of the two wins, it was a good reminder to the players that there was still plenty of work to do to secure a home semi-final, and there was no room for a let-up.

"That two-match period was a wake-up call in the right way at the right time, because we didn't lose to Sale or Bristol," added Baxter.

"We had also had that bit of a break and a rest, so they were good games to get us back up to speed.

"You can't say we didn't work for the full 80 minutes against Sale and Bristol, because we won both games by having to work very hard through the whole of the second half.

"That was the period when we were giving up interception tries, and a lot was being made about that.

"We did give up some soft tries in that period, but in the Bristol game, one of them occurred when the ball bounced in an incredible way for the player to be able to pluck it up, which might never happen again.

"Another thing we learnt from those two games – and this is a good lesson for me from a coaching perspective – is that Sale and Bristol actually did things in those games that were totally different to how they had been playing in what you would call regulation league games.

"We were stacking together a lot of wins at that stage, scoring a lot of tries and points and playing really well, and I actually think they took a bit of a gamble against us, and they started to fly up on the outside, looking to try and cut us off and genuinely looking for interceptions and looking for pressure moments out wide, when that hadn't actually been in their defensive structures all season.

"That did create a little bit of pressure for us, but it also taught us a few lessons, about making sure we played what we saw right in front of us, and not just blindly expecting what an opposition team would do.

"What was really good was we learnt through the course of those games what was happening, and it also meant we could adjust really well at half-time, and it just showed the guys could take on board messages and learn and adapt through the duration of a match, and that was hugely important for us for that to be able to happen."

The game against Bristol had come at a major cost to the Chiefs, with locks Mitch Lees and Jonny Hill both picking up significant knee injuries, with Hill's problem sadly seeing him miss the rest of the campaign, while Waldrom suffered a broken hand, and full-back Phil Dollman was forced to drop out on the eve of the next game with a hamstring injury.

It was a match in which the Chiefs had enjoyed around 75 per cent territory and possession.

"We had to work exceptionally hard for a large part of that game to make the win happen, and that ultimately cost us bodies, and that frustrated me," explained Baxter. "If you look at the stats from that game, the amount of ball carries we made, and tackles Bristol had to make, we had the top three or four ball carriers, and they had the top three or four tacklers in the whole of the Premiership that weekend."

Baxter's comments are certainly borne out by the OPTA statistics for that weekend.

Michele Campagnaro coasts in against Harlequins for an incredible eighth try in six matches for the Chiefs

Waldrom made 30 carries during the match, the most by any player since OPTA began recording that data in 2008-09.

He was followed by Cowan-Dickie on 21, with Nowell (17), Dave Dennis (16) and Ollie Devoto (15) not far behind.

Bristol, meanwhile, boasted the top three for most tackles in round 19, with Sam Jeffries' 28 putting him ahead of team-mates Mark Sorenson (27) and Nick Fenton-Wells (24).

After two escapes against teams they were expected to beat, Baxter was looking forward to the Good Friday trip to Harlequins because of the challenge it would offer his players.

He hated saying it, but speaking after the Bristol game on *BBC Radio Devon*, Baxter commented: "It sounds awful, but whether the last two home games have been enough of an exciting challenge to really get the guys focused, I don't know.

"Going to Quins on a Friday, having not played that well and knowing our backs are against the wall a little bit, might be just what we need, and might be something that really does focus us very, very clearly mentally."

It certainly had the desired effect as Chiefs turned in another superb performance on the road against a Quins side who, in the first half, played some of the best rugby I had seen them produce in a few seasons.

It was one of my favourite matches of the regular Premiership season to commentate on, because it was a game you just could not take your eyes off, and it was a fantastic spectacle for the neutral. There were also some wonderful tries to savour.

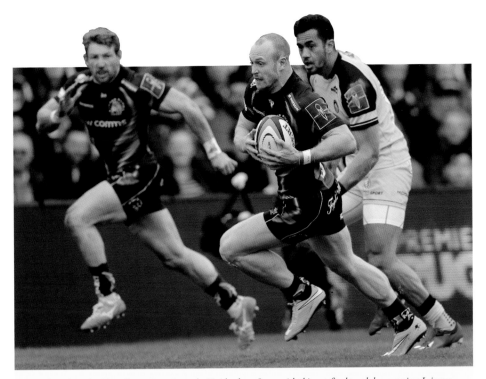

James Short shows his liking for scoring tries at the Twickenham Stoop with this cup final touchdown against Leicester

Exeter had managed an incredible 62-24 victory at the Twickenham Stoop in the closing stages of the previous season, when they made it a totally forgettable farewell home game for Quins' director of rugby Conor O'Shea before he headed off to take charge of the Italian national team.

No-one was expecting a repeat of that against a Quins side sitting in the sixth and final Champions Cup spot, only ahead of Northampton by virtue of having more wins, and desperate for a victory themselves, and having only lost once at home in the Premiership all season – to Leicester at the end of February.

But with the lead over second-place Saracens still only a point, and with the Londoners opting to rest a few of their stars for their own difficult trip to face Northampton at Stadium MK, this was a real opportunity for Exeter to open up a bit of a gap over the reigning champions in the table, and take a little bit of pressure off the final two matches of the regular season against Northampton and Gloucester.

Quins fielded all of their international stars, with Joe Marler, James Horwill, Chris Robshaw, Danny Care, Jamie Roberts, Mike Brown and Marland Yarde all present and correct, and the way they started the game suggested Exeter were going to be in for a tough evening, unless they could lift their performance considerably from the Sale and Bristol games.

Only three minutes had gone when the hosts created the space for big No.8 Mat Luamanu to cross in the corner, but Exeter's riposte was swift, with a penalty from Slade and a try by Ewers in what was an inspired performance by the big man.

Lachie Turner kicks ahead and is about to race past Nick Evans to score a wonderful individual try in the Premiership clash at Harlequins

Nick Evans levelled matters with a penalty in what was proving to be a pulsating battle for supremacy, but the Chiefs scored again when Short won an aerial battle against Brown after Slade's high, hanging kick, and then spun the ball wide to Woodburn, whose delightful back-of-the-hand pass sent Campagnaro over for a converted try.

Exeter leaked a soft penalty just before the break to leave them with a 15-11 advantage, but the curse of the interception try struck again as former New Zealand All Black Evans raced away after gleefully accepting Devoto's misplaced pass.

Trailing 16-15, Exeter turned down one kickable penalty to go for the corner, but messed up the line-out. However, another chance from further out was slotted superbly by Slade and Exeter were back in front.

The Chiefs squandered a possible two-on-one opportunity down the right flank soon after, and it appeared particularly costly when Evans kicked another penalty to make it 19-18 to Quins.

But, before you knew it, Exeter had put the game out of sight with three tries after moments of magic, good fortune and sheer brilliance.

Former Australian international full-back Lachie Turner, only playing because of Dollman's injury, was released at pace by Short, and he intelligently kicked the ball over Evans' head and won the race for the touchdown.

Steenson converted that, and the bonus-point try two minutes later when Jack Maunder miscued his box kick after suffering cramp as he kicked the ball, but it bounced invitingly into the hands of the onrushing Slade, who again chipped over the last line of defence to score beneath the posts.

The third try, three minutes from time, was Turner's fifth in three games against Quins during the season, and again followed a kick into the back field, and once more the bounce of the ball was kind.

Quins managed a late consolation try through Dutch-born Scotland international winger Tim Visser, but they were left shaking their heads at the end at how well they had played in parts and still lost the game 39-26.

"Harlequins were good for a large part of that game, and we were having to battle and battle, and to come through like we did was fantastic," said Baxter.

"Lachie's first try was exceptional, as was his all-round game that day.

"Some of his defence was fantastic, the way he held things together, and for him to pick up an injury soon after that game was tough for him, because he would have been hard to leave out in the run-in, the way he was playing. He was genuinely performing really, really well.

"We also got a bit of a lucky try from Jack Maunder's kick when he was cramping up, but it again showed me that, when you are 'on it' as a team, the other team are going to have to do something special to beat you.

"Quins had all of their internationals back and it was pretty much the strongest team they could put out on the field, and by the end of the 80 minutes we had dealt with that scenario really, really well."

Exeter had equalled a Premiership-best six successive bonus-point wins with their five-pointer against Quins, but it was not the last time they were going to trouble the record books before the season was out.

ANGLO-WELSH CUP
SEMI-FINAL – EXETER CHIEFS 24 HARLEQUINS 7
(Sunday, March 12, Sandy Park)

Chiefs: L Turner; M Jess, O Devoto (T Hendrickson 70), S Hill, M Bodilly; J Simmonds (W Hooley 75), S Townsend (H Thomas 64); B Moon (B Keast 70), S Malton (E Taione 57), H Williams (M Low 57); O Atkins, D Welch (J Hill 51); T Johnson (D Ewers 51), J Salvi (capt), S Simmonds.

Harlequins: R Chisholm; C Walker, J Marchant, M Hopper (M Yarde 57), Alofa Alofa; R Jackson (J Lang 57), L Jones (C Waters 65); M Lambert (O Evans 57), J Gray (R Buchanan 52-64), A Jones (M Shields 47); G Merrick, C Matthews (R Hodson 64); G Naupou (S South 16), D Ward (capt), M Luamanu.

Chiefs: Tries – Turner, Bodilly, Salvi, S Simmonds; Conversions – J Simmonds (2).
Harlequins: Try – Waters; Conversion – Lang.

HT: 14-0. **Referee:** Dan Jones (Wales). **Attendance:** 9,419.

FINAL – EXETER CHIEFS 12 LEICESTER TIGERS 16

(Sunday, March 19, Twickenham Stoop)

Chiefs: L Turner; M Jess, M Bodilly, S Hill (T Hendrickson 71), J Short; J Simmonds (W Hooley 71), J Maunder (H Thomas 70); C Rimmer (B Keast 70), S Malton (E Taione 64), G Holmes (J Owlett 65); O Atkins (S Skinner 56), D Welch; D Ewers (T Johnson 70), J Salvi (capt), S Simmonds (E Taione 46-51).

Leicester: G Worth; P Betham, M Tait (capt, M Smith 78), J Roberts, T Brady; F Burns (O Williams 63-70), J Kitto (B White 70); E Genge (M Rizzo 75), G McGuigan (T Youngs 70), F Balmain (G Bateman 51); H Wells, G Kitchener (D Barrow 65); M Williams, H Thacker, L McCaffrey (L Hamilton 67).

Chiefs: Tries – Short, S Simmonds; Conversion – Hooley.
Leicester: Try – Brady; Conversion – Burns; Penalties – Burns (3).

HT: 5-16. **Referee:** Tom Foley (RFU). **Attendance:** 6,834.

PREMIERSHIP

ROUND 18 – EXETER CHIEFS 30 SALE SHARKS 25

(Saturday, March 25, Sandy Park)

Chiefs: P Dollman; J Nowell (J Short 78), I Whitten, O Devoto, O Woodburn; H Slade, S Townsend (J Maunder 54); B Moon (C Rimmer 59), L Cowan-Dickie (J Yeandle 59), H Williams (T Francis 59); M Lees, G Parling (J Hill 63); K Horstmann (S Simmonds 67), D Armand (capt), T Waldrom. Replacement (not used): J Simmonds.

Sale: M Haley; D Solomona, S James, M Jennings (S Bedlow 58), B McGuigan (J Charnley 74); AJ MacGinty, M Phillips (J Mitchell 69); R Harrison (J Flynn 70), R Webber, H Aulika (K Longbottom 63); B Evans (G Nott 69), A Ostrikov (L Pearce 63); C Nield, T Curry (B Curry 58), J Beaumont (capt).

Chiefs: Tries – Horstmann, Cowan-Dickie, Woodburn, Armand; Conversions – Slade (2); Penalties – Slade (2).
Sale: Try – Solomona; Conversion – MacGinty; Penalties – MacGinty (6).

HT: 12-19. **Referee:** Craig Maxwell-Keys (RFU). **Attendance:** 10,924.

ROUND 19 – EXETER CHIEFS 38 BRISTOL 34

(Saturday, April 8, Sandy Park)

Chiefs: P Dollman; J Nowell (M Campagnaro 60), I Whitten, O Devoto (G Steenson 60), O Woodburn; H Slade, J Maunder (S Townsend 68); B Moon (C Rimmer 52), L Cowan-Dickie (J Yeandle 77), H Williams (G Holmes 52); M Lees (G Parling 39), J Hill (D Ewers 43); D Dennis, D Armand (capt), T Waldrom.

Bristol: J Woodward; R Edwards, W Hurrell, G Henson, J Tovey; B Searle, A Mathewson (R Williams 60); R Bevington (J O'Connell 36), M Jones (capt, M Crumpton 56), G Cortes (J Ford-Robinson ht); J Phillips (B Glynn 67), M Sorenson; S Jeffries, J Lam (N Fenton-Wells 12), M Eadie. Replacements (not used): J Newey, C Amesbury.

Chiefs: Tries – Woodburn, Parling, Whitten, Waldrom (2); Conversions – Slade (4), Steenson; Penalty – Slade.
Bristol: Tries – Hurrell, Woodward, Henson, Eadie; Conversions – Henson (4); Penalties – Henson (2).

HT: 17-24. **Referee:** Tom Foley (RFU). **Attendance:** 12,232.

ROUND 20 – HARLEQUINS 26 EXETER CHIEFS 39

(Friday, April 14, Twickenham Stoop)

Harlequins: M Brown; M Yarde, J Marchant (Alofa Alofa 67), J Roberts, T Visser; N Evans (T Swiel 70), D Care (capt); J Marler, R Buchanan (J Gray 5-13, 70), K Sinckler (W Collier 61); C Matthews (G Merrick 63), J Horwill; C Robshaw, L Wallace, M Luamanu. Replacements (not used): M Lambert, D Ward, C Mulchrone.

Chiefs: L Turner; O Woodburn, M Campagnaro (G Steenson 61), O Devoto (S Hill 57), J Short; H Slade, J Maunder (S Townsend 69); C Rimmer (B Moon 50), J Yeandle (capt, S Malton 67), G Holmes (T Francis 50); D Dennis, G Parling (O Atkins 77); D Ewers, D Armand, K Horstmann (J Salvi 57).

Harlequins: Tries – Luamanu, Evans, Visser; Conversion – Swiel; Penalties – Evans (3).
Chiefs: Tries – Ewers, Campagnaro, Turner (2), Slade; Conversions – Slade, Steenson (3); Penalties – Slade (2).

HT: 11-15. **Referee:** Wayne Barnes (RFU). **Attendance:** 14,800.

Jack Nowell congratulates Olly Woodburn on one of his two tries in the Chiefs' biggest ever win over Northampton Saints

CHAPTER 9

Record Breakers

PREMIERSHIP TABLE							
	P	**W**	**D**	**L**	**F**	**A**	**Pts**
Wasps	22	17	1	4	693	502	84
EXETER	**22**	**15**	**3**	**4**	**667**	**452**	**84**
Saracens	22	16	1	5	579	345	77
Leicester	22	14	0	8	567	445	66
Bath	22	12	0	10	486	440	59
Harlequins	22	11	0	11	532	526	52
Northampton	22	10	0	12	476	490	52
Newcastle	22	10	0	12	430	581	49
Gloucester	22	7	2	13	533	537	46
Sale	22	7	1	14	471	595	40
Worcester	22	5	2	15	466	662	33
Bristol	22	3	0	19	382	707	20

APRIL

Saturday 29   AP   W   Exeter Chiefs 36   Northampton Saints 12

MAY

Saturday 6   AP   W   Gloucester 20   Exeter Chiefs 34

Points available 10 – points taken 10

WITH Exeter's place in the semi-finals safely secured, it was just a case now of sorting out whether they would be at home in the last four, and who they would be playing.

Saracens showed their quality by winning at Northampton Saints last time out, despite naming a weakened team, but they failed to pick up a losing bonus point.

It meant the Chiefs suddenly had a two-point cushion over the Londoners, and nine points from their last two games would guarantee a home last-four clash with them.

Top spot was also not out of the question at that stage either, with Wasps only five points ahead – or effectively six, given the fact they had won three more matches than Chiefs and that would be the deciding factor if they finished tied on points.

Jack Nowell shares a lovely moment with JP Doyle after the referee calls for the television match official to decide whether the grounding was good for the Cornishman's try against Northampton. It was!

Wasps had a very tough run-in, with a trip to Harlequins, who were still chasing a top-six finish and place in the 2017-18 Champions Cup, and intriguingly, a home game with Saracens, whose other fixture looked like a 'gimme' five-pointer at home to Bristol.

Regardless of all of the permutations, Exeter still had a very tough job to do themselves, with Northampton at home and Gloucester away still to come.

Like Quins, both were still chasing down a spot in Europe's top-tier competition the following season, and Saints still had a very outside chance of getting into the top four at the expense of their arch-rivals Leicester.

However, speaking to media colleagues from Northampton before the game, they sensed the Saints were targeting what they felt would be a winner-takes-all clash at home to Harlequins on the final day of the season, and they were confident it would very much be Exeter's day.

Northampton arrived in Devon off the back of three narrow, heart-breaking defeats, at home to Leicester and Saracens and away to Wasps, but their cause was not helped by the absence of some key personnel in France international No.8 Louis Picamoles, Wales and British and Irish Lions winger George North, fly-half Stephen Myler and England back rower Tom Wood. However, they still fielded a side full of internationals.

The Chiefs themselves were without half-backs Jack Maunder and Henry Slade due to injury niggles, but they welcomed the return to the starting XV of Gareth Steenson after his hamstring problems, and Welford Road hero Stu Townsend.

Once again, Exeter underlined their title credentials by producing one of their best home displays of the season, scoring six tries in their 36-12 success – their biggest ever victory over the Saints.

The records did not end there though. They set a Premiership best with their seventh successive bonus-point win – a phenomenal achievement given how tough the league was – surpassing Leicester's six in 2012.

They also posted another league record of securing a try-scoring bonus point in eight consecutive games, with the Wasps draw, when they bagged five tries, tagged on to the front end of that seven-match winning run.

The margin of victory could have been even greater, as they had tries by winger Jack Nowell (not grounding the ball properly) and the livewire Townsend (knock-on) disallowed by referee JP Doyle, and saw one or two other good scoring chances go begging.

Two features of several of the Chiefs' recent home games had been conceding first, and giving up what was almost becoming a regulation interception try.

Those two elements combined after only five minutes, with Saints fly-half JJ Hanrahan picking off a pass from Exeter centre Ollie Devoto to run in under the posts, and add the conversion himself.

It turned out to only be a minor blip for Exeter, though, as they dominated territory and possession in the first half, which was played in a strong, gusting wind.

However, it took them until just past the half-hour mark to get their noses in front.

Don Armand muscled his way over in the 27th minute, with Steenson converting to level the scores, and within 60 seconds of Saints losing Samoan winger Ken Pisi to a yellow card for a deliberate knock-on of Olly Woodburn's pass in the 32nd minute, Townsend sniped down the blindside off a driving maul to attack the spot where Pisi would have been, and sent Woodburn in for a try in the corner, and Exeter led 12-7 at the break.

A storming start to the second half saw Woodburn make an initial incision on the left, before the ball was spun to the right, where Irish centre Ian Whitten gathered Steenson's bounce pass, brushed off a couple of tackles and crossed the whitewash.

Irish centre Ian Whitten powers away from the Northampton defence at Sandy Park

Sam Hill evades the tackle of Juan Pablo Estelles to grab Exeter's fifth try of the contest against Northampton

The try that confirmed the bonus-point record came just before the hour mark – and it was a stunning one, too, at the end of a great attacking move. It was fitting it came from young Cornishman Nowell as he went into the game celebrating his inclusion in the Lions squad to tour New Zealand in the summer and finally got the touchdown his efforts in the match deserved.

Scrum-half Will Chudley came off the bench for his first action in three months after surgery on both of his shoulders, but Saints – who lost England forward Courtney Lawes early on to concussion – continued to look dangerous until two tries in the final 11 minutes killed them off.

Replacement centre Sam Hill got the first after a sweet sidestep, and Woodburn the second after he was unselfishly put in by Nowell, with Steenson and Joe Simmonds slotting a conversion apiece, before Ahsee Tuala managed a late consolation try for Northampton.

It was 25-year-old former Bath winger Woodburn's second try of the match and his 11th of the season, with 10 of those in the league, and it was another performance that made Eddie Jones' decision not to include him in the England squad for the summer tour to Argentina even more baffling, especially when he had picked 19-year-old Joe Cokanasiga – who had spent the season playing in the Championship for London Irish – ahead of him.

Woodburn was also presented with the Exeter Chiefs Supporters' Club Player of the Season award after the game.

"It is a tough one on Olly not going on the trip, because he has fallen into a bracket of players who they have probably overlooked ahead of developing youngsters," commented Exeter backs coach Ali Hepher after the game.

"To be fair to Olly, each week he just puts his head down and concentrates on what he does well, and he is coming through really strongly.

"His work rate off the ball is unseen, he chases hard off the ball, he wins ball in the air, and he is a big, strong, powerful, quick guy, and that is what you want from your wingers. He is improving all of the time, and I think there is more to come from him."

What made a great day even more special, and rubbed plenty more salt into injury-hit Northampton's gaping wounds, was the news that Harlequins had picked up an incredible 32-13 bonus-point win at home to Wasps in Nick Evans' farewell home game before hanging up his boots, and he celebrated in style with a 22-point haul with his boot.

Suddenly the Chiefs were level on points with Wasps at the top of the table, and it created the prospect of maybe a home semi-final against Leicester, rather than Saracens.

The Saints, meanwhile, now found themselves outside the top six and three points behind Quins going into their head-to-head on the final day of the regular season.

Prop Ben Moon goes over for his first ever Premiership try for Exeter in the win at Gloucester

Exeter headed off to Kingsholm to face Gloucester in confident mood after seven straight Premiership wins, and having triumphed on three of their last five league visits to what can be a very intimidating ground.

However, hopes of finishing in top spot had been slightly diminished by Saracens again resting players for their trip to Wasps, though understandably so, given they had their Champions Cup final against Clermont Auvergne in Edinburgh the following weekend.

They had made it quite clear that they did not mind whether they were home or away in the semi-finals, and who could argue with that approach, given they had won the Premiership and European Cup double the previous season?

The Cherry and Whites' dreams of a top-six finish were now over after their 44-20 drubbing at Bath the previous week, but they still had hopes of securing seventh place and a play-off for a Champions Cup spot.

They faced a bit of a dilemma when it came to team selection, as six days later they had a Challenge Cup final against Stade Francais at Murrayfield, the winners of which would also gain a place in European rugby's top tier, but director of rugby David Humphreys opted to select a near full-strength side.

Baxter made six changes, partly due to injuries, and gave a first Premiership start since October 8 – which was ironically also against Gloucester – to Australian openside flanker Julian Salvi, and to lock Ollie Atkins, who had not kicked off a league game since the visit to Saracens on January 7.

It was another humdinger of a contest in front of a sell-out crowd, and when they trailed 15-6 it looked as if Exeter's proud 14-match unbeaten run might be coming to an end.

Ian Whitten picks a hole in the Gloucester defence to score his sixth try of the season

Gloucester survived an early scare, when James Short fumbled a pass from Devoto with the line at his mercy, to score a try after only eight minutes through openside flanker Lewis Ludlow following an inside ball by England winger Jonny May, and captain Greig Laidlaw kicked the conversion on his last Kingsholm appearance before his summer move to Clermont Auvergne.

Exeter skipper Steenson (2) and Laidlaw exchanged penalties to make it 10-6, before Steenson inexplicably missed a third effort from virtually in front of the posts.

Two minutes later, May intercepted a pass by Steenson on halfway and raced in for another try, and even though Laidlaw's conversion was wide, Gloucester led 15-6.

It was not going well for Exeter. When they were awarded another penalty midway inside the home half, they turned down the shot at goal and opted to kick to the corner, and even though the subsequent line-out drive started well enough, Gloucester regrouped well and secured a crucial turnover.

However, pundits had learnt many times over the course of the season that you write the Chiefs off at your peril.

Whitten bagged his sixth try of the season after a neat midfield interchange with Steenson and some poor home tackling, with Steenson adding the extras.

Whitten almost gifted Charlie Sharples yet another interception try soon after, but he got back well to tap tackle the former England winger, and the Chiefs reached the break only trailing 15-13.

May had a try ruled out for a knock-on by James Hook, before Exeter delivered a one-two in the space of five devastating minutes for Gloucester that the great Muhammad Ali would have been proud of.

After a series of forward drives, loose-head prop Ben Moon took Townsend's pass to dive over like a winger in the left-hand corner for his first ever Premiership try, and that was soon followed by Short with his 14th of the campaign, with Steenson improving both for a 27-15 lead.

The excellent May stepped his way past England team-mate Nowell like he was not even there to bag his second try of the game as Gloucester refused to accept defeat, but Exeter came roaring back, with replacement scrum-half Chudley sniping over beside the posts after a period of intense Chiefs pressure for the bonus-point try, with Steenson adding the simple conversion.

Exeter had extended their two Premiership records to eight successive bonus-point victories, and nine consecutive league matches where they had registered a try-scoring bonus point.

However, they missed out on top spot by a whisker to Wasps, whose own bonus-point victory over Saracens, in a game that controversially kicked off 15 minutes later than all the others due to crowd congestion, secured them number one seeding in the play-offs, by virtue of their 17 wins compared to Exeter's 15, with both finishing on 84 points.

It meant a semi-final line-up of Wasps against Leicester, and Exeter versus Saracens.

Baxter was delighted for Moon, who was one of the so-called 'Originals' from the club's Championship-winning campaign.

"He had a ding-dong battle with Carl Rimmer all the way through the season, and for a guy who has been with us for so long to keep going and keep improving and keep working hard at what he wanted to do is a big quality, and he has been really important for us," said Baxter.

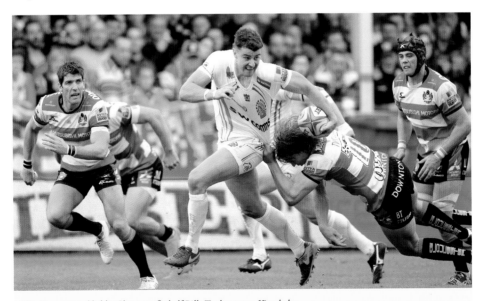

Ollie Devoto is tackled by Gloucester fly-half Billy Twelvetrees at Kingsholm

"You can go through guys one at a time and when you stop and break their performances down, you see how hard they have worked.

"I don't think people quite realise, when we talk about ball-in-play time, how much higher we are than nearly every other Premiership team.

"A game involving Exeter Chiefs can sometimes have the ball actually being played in that match seven to 10 minutes more compared to other Premiership games, and that is a physical challenge.

"You have got to have some really good qualities, when the ball has been on the field for five minutes and everyone wants to put their hands on their knees and stop, to be the guy that keeps going, and Ben is one of those top forwards who thrives in that kind of environment, and he showed those qualities through the run-in."

Two recurring themes in after-match interviews with Baxter during this period were interception tries, and Exeter's growing injury list.

May's touchdown for Gloucester was incredibly the seventh try the Chiefs had conceded in that manner in only six games, and Baxter admitted it was an issue the Exeter coaching staff wrestled with over this spell.

"It was a really interesting challenge, and we talked about it a lot as coaches," explained Baxter.

"We asked ourselves: 'Do we want to make as big a deal about it as everyone else seems to be doing, and become a team where we create a bit of doubt and actually don't make passes?

"Because, at the same time as we were giving up these interception tries, we had been in a period where we had put together the biggest ever run of Premiership bonus-point wins, so we had to decide how we were going to approach it.

"We talked about some of the things that led to interceptions, so where someone passed blind, and was almost giving the pass because they assumed there was going to be space, we obviously worked with those individuals and told them that they needed to be making a better decision than that.

"Where the opposition had changed their defence and had gambled and gone for interceptions, we talked about that a little bit, but when we analysed those games, what people never appreciated was that in plenty of those matches, teams had gone for interceptions where they hadn't come off and we had scored.

"We were always a fair bit more comfortable with it than people on the outside were.

"We were frustrated by giving up the interception scores, but we were also scoring tries by playing in that manner and keeping the ball on the field and moving opposition defences and challenging them with those last, flat passes.

"We didn't feel great about it, because you never want to give them up, but we were okay about it. The interception tries weren't all created by one reason. There wasn't one thing that tied them altogether, so we just dealt with them as individual scenarios.

"When you are a team that is going well, and particularly at home, and a team decide to gamble for things in the hope that they will come off, because they feel that will give them the best chance of winning, that is different to you creating your own problems, and that is what happened in a few of those interception tries."

The other big issue was the number of injuries the Chiefs were picking up, and on the face of it were threatening to scupper their hopes of winning the title.

The Bristol game saw Mitch Lees, Jonny Hill, Thomas Waldrom and Phil Dollman all injured; Quins accounted for Jack Maunder and Henry Slade; against Northampton it was Dave Ewers, Greg Holmes, Dave Dennis, Lachie Turner and Don Armand; while Olly Woodburn (hamstring) and Julian Salvi got crocked at Gloucester.

All of a sudden Exeter were starting to look a little bit thin on the ground in some areas, and their deep squad was being tested to the full.

The injuries also occurred at a time when they were facing three tough fixtures with which to end their season, but Baxter felt to come through them with a maximum 15-point haul, when so many frontline personnel were sidelined, said huge amounts about the character of his squad.

"Harlequins, Gloucester and Northampton were all fighting for something, and in a way that was good because it meant every game had quite a lot on it," he said.

"This part of the season highlighted the strength and the quality of the squad, because we made changes game by game.

"We talked about using guys on the bench, and using different players and different combinations to keep things ticking over and fresh and alive.

"With that number of injured players, you have got to give so much credit to our conditioning and medical team because, as we were losing players during the season, you look at how many came back to play important parts for us.

"Olly Woodburn came back to play in the final, Tom Waldrom was back to play in the semi-final, Mitch Lees returned to take up a bench spot in both games and Jonny Hill was just slightly behind Mitch and maybe could have been there if we had needed him.

"A huge number of players worked exceptionally hard with the medical team, who worked wonders really.

"We showed incredible character in all of those last three games, and they ticked so many boxes in that regard.

"We brought in players who played fantastically well, added energy, kept us going forward, and kept other guys fresh, and you can't underestimate how big those games were for us."

You had to feel for the unfortunate Ewers, who missed the first two months of the season with a knee injury, worked hard to get back fit and then picked up another problem away to Bordeaux just before Christmas. Then, having returned in time to play in the Anglo-Welsh Cup semi-final and final, and making his first Premiership start of the season against Harlequins, he suffered yet another bad knee injury against Northampton, which would not only see him miss the Premiership final but rule him out of the start of the 2017-18 campaign.

This was all off the back of missing a large part of the previous season with injury.

Ewers is such a talent that, given a good run of games, it would surely be hard for Jones to turn down his claims for a spot in his England squad, but luck was deserting him.

"There are two ways you can look at your whole season. You can base it around your injury issues, or around all the opportunities that are created because of them and that players take," said Baxter.

"Jack Nowell being out for quite a long time was a blow for us, but then you look at how James Short performed.

"It is tough, and it was dreadful for Dave getting injured during the season because he is an important player for us, but then you look at the opportunity it created for someone like Kai Horstmann, who has played an awful lot of Premiership rugby, and a lot of that was at Worcester where, to be fair, he spent a large part of his career scrabbling around at the wrong end of the table, and all of a sudden he has played in semi-finals and finals and is a Premiership winner."

Despite being aged 35, Horstmann had an excellent season – arguably his best for the Chiefs – playing in 17 of the 24 games, and he was rewarded with a new one-year contract.

Baxter added: "I always like to say to all the guys who pick up bad injuries that, as annoying and disappointing as it is, the way professional rugby players need to look at it now is, every game you don't play is a game you can add on to the end of your career, because for professional sportsmen now it is almost more about the number of games you play, rather than the number of years, and I think that is how it will be

The Exeter players celebrate securing a home semi-final against Saracens with victory at Gloucester

with Dave, and you will see him have a number of very good seasons based on a period now where, he is obviously trying to get his knee right, but he can actually work on his whole body and whole frame in very positive ways as well."

So after 22 matches, Exeter had secured the home semi-final they wanted, but they faced the formidable challenge of a Saracens side who the week before the eagerly-anticipated Sandy Park showdown had won the European Champions Cup for the second year running by beating Clermont Auvergne 28-17 at Murrayfield.

ROUND 21

EXETER CHIEFS 36 NORTHAMPTON SAINTS 12

(Saturday, April 29, Sandy Park)

Chiefs: L Turner; J Nowell, I Whitten, O Devoto (S Hill 55), O Woodburn; G Steenson (J Simmonds 70), S Townsend (W Chudley 52); C Rimmer (B Moon 49), J Yeandle (capt, L Cowan-Dickie 55), G Holmes (H Williams 6, C Rimmer 74); D Dennis, G Parling; D Ewers (J Salvi 11), D Armand (O Atkins 64), K Horstmann.

Northampton: A Tuala; K Pisi (J-P Estelles 52-79), L Burrell, H Mallinder, B Foden (N Tuitavake 68); JJ Hanrahan, N Groom (L Dickson 59); A Waller (C Ma'afu 57), D Hartley (capt) (M Haywood 59), K Brookes (G Denman 57); C Day (A Ratuniyarawa 58), D Ribbans; C Lawes (S Dickinson 21, C Day 79), J Gibson, T Harrison.

Chiefs: Tries – Armand, Woodburn (2), Whitten, Nowell, S Hill; Conversions – Steenson (2), J Simmonds.
Northampton: Tries – Hanrahan, Tuala; Conversion – Hanrahan.

Yellow Card: Northampton – K Pisi.

HT: 12-7. **Referee:** JP Doyle (RFU). **Attendance:** 12,284.

ROUND 22 – GLOUCESTER 20 EXETER CHIEFS 34

(Saturday, May 6, Kingsholm)

Gloucester: J Hook; C Sharples (O Thorley 56), M Scott (H Trinder 66), M Atkinson, J May; B Twelvetrees, G Laidlaw (capt) (W Heinz 62); P McAllister (Y Thomas 53), R Hibbard (D Dawiduik 72), J Afoa (J Hohneck 66); T Savage (J Thrush 69), M Galarza; F Clarke, L Ludlow (J Rowan 69), B Morgan.

Chiefs: J Nowell; O Woodburn (S Hill 66), I Whitten, O Devoto, J Short; G Steenson (capt), S Townsend (W Chudley 57); B Moon (C Rimmer 57), L Cowan-Dickie (J Yeandle 57), H Williams (T Francis 57); O Atkins (S Skinner 74), G Parling; D Dennis, J Salvi (S Simmonds 23), K Horstmann. Replacement (not used): J Simmonds.

Gloucester: Tries – Ludlow, May (2); Conversion – Laidlaw; Penalty – Laidlaw.
Chiefs: Tries – Whitten, Moon, Short, Chudley; Conversions – Steenson (4); Penalties – Steenson (2).

HT: 15-13. **Referee:** Ian Tempest (RFU). **Attendance:** 16,115.

*Captain Gareth Steenson
and Jack Nowell celebrate
Exeter's first try in the
semi-final in front of top
international referee
Wayne Barnes*

CHAPTER 10

They Think It's All Over.....

Premiership semi-final
Saturday 20   W   Exeter Chiefs 18   Saracens 16

I AM sure there were plenty of people like me inside Sandy Park who thought it really was all over for Exeter Chiefs when replacement Mike Ellery dived over for a try to put Saracens in front with only five minutes remaining.

Exeter had matched their star-studded rivals blow for blow in a fascinating, absorbing semi-final, but as so often happens with great teams – and Saracens undoubtedly fall into that category – they somehow always seem to find a way of getting that crucial score to push them over the winning line.

Sarries have reminded me in recent seasons of the fantastic Arsenal sides in the early part of Arsene Wenger's reign at what was then Highbury, who had the ability to grind out 1-0 victories to kill off the bravest and strongest of challenges from the opposition, even when they were not at their best.

Saracens arrived in Devon as reigning Premiership champions; they had just completed back-to-back Champions Cup triumphs to confirm they were the best team in Europe; they boasted five players selected for the British and Irish Lions tour to New Zealand the following month in their pack of forwards alone, and another in England fly-half Owen Farrell in their back division who had just been named EPCR European Player of the Year.

They had beaten the Chiefs in the 2016 Premiership final; in fact, Exeter had not come out on top of them in their five games since the Devon side had won at Allianz Park in May 2015.

Saracens had thrashed Rob Baxter's men 34-13 when they had met at Sandy Park on the second weekend of the Premiership season. They had also drawn with them in the return fixture in early January, despite playing for 69 minutes with only 14 men after the dismissal of prop Richard Barrington.

They did not seem to mind whether they were home or away in the semi-final either, and why would they?

They had won in Toulon in the European pool stages; they had beaten Munster in Ireland in the Champions Cup quarter-finals; name any venue and they seemed confident of winning.

Exeter, of course, had not lost in the Premiership since October 30; they had set league records for most successive bonus-point wins, and securing a try-bonus point for the longest run of games, and they also had a Lion of their own in Jack Nowell and some excellent other players to boot.

But it was Saracens they were playing and anything other than a win for the Londoners just wasn't meant to be, was it?

Rob Baxter talked a lot about the strength of character his team had shown in the run-in to the end of the season in the previous chapter, and it was again in evidence in spades in the dying moments on this Saturday afternoon.

The Chiefs were awarded a scrum penalty just outside their 22, and with little more than a minute remaining, playing against the best defence in the Premiership by a country mile – Sarries had only conceded 28 tries in 22 matches during the regular season, compared to the 55 shipped by Exeter – they only appeared to have one option, and that was to kick to the corner.

Up stepped Henry Slade, a hugely talented young man who had come in for a lot of criticism, most of it totally unwarranted, since he returned from a broken leg in March 2016.

I remember watching him playing for Plymouth College at Delgany in February 2011, in an Under-18 Daily Mail Cup quarter-final against a Whitgift School side that included a certain Elliot Daly in their ranks, and it was obvious then that a star was in the making.

It was an all-or-nothing kick for Slade, who picked up the ball, took aim with his left foot, and hammered it an amazing 60 metres, with it landing just the right side of the corner flag.

The ground took a collective deep breath as Exeter club captain Jack Yeandle lined up his five-metre line-out throw before picking out Dave Dennis, and as the ball was fed back to 22-year-old Teignmouth lad Sam Simmonds, he was driven over by a marauding mass of black shirts, with referee Wayne Barnes pausing for a second or two to check the grounding before awarding the try.

There was no time to restart the game, Gareth Steenson's conversion miss did not matter, and Exeter had secured a famous victory that sparked some of the most incredible scenes of celebration ever witnessed at Sandy Park, even more so than 12 months before when they had seen off Wasps to book their first ever visit to a Premiership final.

Saracens were totally stunned. The body language and the expressions on their players' faces said it all. The unthinkable for them had happened, and they were going to have to content themselves with just the one trophy from their season – the Champions Cup.

So how important was home advantage in the semi-finals?

Baxter had never made any secret of his desire to secure a last-four game at Sandy Park.

Sam Simmonds has the ball as Exeter drive towards the try line, before Wayne Barnes gives the score, to the obvious delight of the Chiefs' players

The semi-final statistics showed just how hard it was to triumph on the road at that stage of the competition, with only five out of 25 Premiership semi-finals having been won by the away team.

That figure became five out of 27 after Exeter's triumph over Saracens, and Wasps' equally last-gasp 21-20 success over Leicester Tigers at the Ricoh Arena in the other last-four tie.

"Going away in a semi-final is tough, and two very tight games were won by the home team, and it is hard to argue against the results being the other way round if the home sides had been away from home," admitted Baxter.

It was also felt by many that, if Exeter were going to win the Premiership, they were better off meeting Saracens in a home semi-final than at Twickenham, where many of the Londoners' players were so comfortable and used to playing.

"When I was talking to people outside of the playing group, I have to admit that was what I felt as well, and that was why we wanted to finish second in the table," revealed Baxter.

"The home semi-final is important to give you the best chance to win, but it is important for the club as well, because you bring the game to your supporters, and financially, the difference between a home and away semi-final is like chalk and cheese.

"You are pretty much making a small fortune out of that home fixture, and the overall package of what you can create as a rugby club and a business is obviously driven by huge things like that.

"We also genuinely felt we could go well against Saracens. We felt we had an idea of how we could challenge them, and talking amongst ourselves as a coaching staff, if it ended up being Saracens at our place in the semi, that wasn't the worst thing in the world."

This might surprise a lot of people, but the Chiefs' coaches also discussed before the game how they would react to a victory over Saracens, with such a quick turnaround before the Twickenham final seven days later.

"It is important as coaches to prepare yourself for wins and losses, and we actually talked as a coaching group that, if we do beat Saracens, how quickly can we leave that game behind?" explained Baxter.

"Saracens had won the European Cup and done the double the previous year, and were kind of going into the semi-final as everyone's favourites, even though they had to come away in the semi-final, as it had not been an issue for them before. We said that, if we do win this game, what are we going to put in place to make sure it gets left behind going into the final, and it doesn't become our biggest performance?"

Saracens' apparent contentment with playing away from home in the last four, coming to a ground where they had won on five of their seven visits since Exeter were in the Premiership, showed great confidence, and some might say arrogance, but Baxter stressed they had not used that to help motivate their players.

"We didn't use the opposition a lot as a motivating factor for us during the season," he said. "Sometimes you can, and I don't think there is anything wrong with that, but the season wasn't about the opposition. We made sure it was about us and we became very focused on ourselves.

"All we ever talked about with the players was what are we going to do about the game collectively and individually? How can we drive this agenda today? How can you, as an individual, make things happen?

"We did our preparation on Saracens, by saying 'this guy is a dangerous ball carrier, or this guy might do this, or this is their pattern of play', but we didn't over-focus on them, and we didn't use the fact that they were double champions, or were comfortable going away from home, or that they had put out a relatively weak team at Wasps the week before their European final. We didn't talk to the players about that being a driver for us at all, because I don't think that was the right thing.

"To be fair, in a lot of ways, because they only lost to us in the last seconds of the game, you could say Saracens virtually got everything right in their preparation – to rest up before they went to Wasps, they won the European Cup final, and until the last line-out of the game, they were beating us."

One huge benefit to Exeter going into the semi-final though was the fact that, as much as they would have loved to have been in a European Cup final, they had a weekend off to recharge their batteries after the game at Gloucester, whereas Saracens were slugging it out in a very physically-draining match against Clermont Auvergne.

"Without doubt, the week's rest in comparison to playing such a big game as Saracens did, favours one side. You can't say anything other than that," said Baxter.

"You have got to give Saracens great credit for the game being like it was, because in a lot of ways they did enough, and we had to play exceptionally well that day.

"When we broke the match down, we were probably a little bit frustrated over what gave them their last piece of field position that allowed them to score their late try, but overall, we got huge parts of that game right.

"Was it a moment of inspiration that won us the game?

"Yes and no. Henry's kick to the corner was inspirational, but the scrum before it always looked like it was going to be a penalty to us, and if you look at the quality of the drive from the line-out for the match-winning try, it never looked like we were going to get stopped.

"It was hugely dynamic, and there were penalties coming in from all over the place by Saracens in their attempts to try and stop it. It would have been interesting to see whether the referee would have gone back for a penalty, but as it was, it was a try, so it didn't matter.

"That result was in us. We were playing at such a level and with such intensity that the game wasn't suddenly a massive step up for us.

"The performances we were putting in against good sides over the last three or four games leading into the semi-final, we were already up at that level, and emotionally and physically we were there.

"It was always going to be a huge game, and it was always going to be a challenge for both sides, and it showed that if we had not been at the right intensity individually and collectively, we would not have been anywhere near winning that game.

"If we had scrummaged that last scrum individually, we wouldn't have won the penalty, but because the eight guys scrummaged collectively, they made it a weapon for us.

"That showed the lessons we had learnt over the course of the season. Our set piece became a weapon for us. It didn't become something that was nice and tidy and looked alright, it was actually something that felt good, and I think the scrum at the end of the game was a perfect example of that."

The OPTA statistics once again confirmed how hard Exeter had worked to achieve their success, with Saracens boasting the top four tacklers on semi-final weekend, with Schalk Burger and Vincent Koch both on 24, and Billy Vunipola and Duncan Taylor on 21.

"If you look at the stats for the two semi-finals, we had all of the top carriers, and they had all of the top tacklers, and I know Saracens don't mind that, but it does show you how hard we went after that game, and how hard we were prepared to work," said Baxter.

"We showed all the qualities that give you the opportunity to win a game. In a lot of ways, it was no different to a number of other games. It was just a bigger, tougher, harder match against better opposition, but the fundamentals of what we had to show were very similar to a lot of the wins that had progressed us to that point."

Exeter were boosted before kick-off by the return from injury of several key men, including Don Armand, Thomas Waldrom, Phil Dollman and Mitch Lees, who was on the bench.

James Short also played against his old club, in the absence of hamstring victim Olly Woodburn.

Saracens were forced to make one change from their European final-winning side, with skipper Brad Barritt ruled out by a leg injury and replaced by Scotland international Duncan Taylor at centre, with Farrell taking over the captain's armband.

What followed was an epic game of rugby from start to finish, and was labelled by many as one of the best ever Premiership semi-finals.

Sarries suffered two early blows, with the loss inside the first 11 minutes of flanker Michael Rhodes and winger Chris Ashton to injury, with the latter playing his last game for the club before moving to Toulon.

Farrell and Exeter skipper Steenson exchanged two penalties apiece to leave it at 6-6 at the break, but the Chiefs still had the wind to come in their favour.

The brutality of the game showed no signs of letting up in the second half, with Sarries' Mako Vunipola and Exeter's Dave Dennis both heading off for head injury assessments after the England prop's huge hit on the Australian.

It was Exeter who scored the game's opening try. Geoff Parling and Ollie Devoto carried well before Stu Townsend sniped for the line and Jack Nowell finished off, leaving his England colleague Billy Vunipola flat footed to squeeze over in the scorebox corner. He again showed his liking for scoring tries against Saracens with his third in four matches, and when Steenson converted superbly from the touchline, the Chiefs led 13-6.

There were some huge hits in the semi-final, as this tackle by Jack Nowell on his England and British and Irish Lions team-mate Maro Itoje demonstrates

Jack Nowell puts Exeter in front for the first time in the semi-final with this touchdown

Exeter scrum-half Stuart Townsend feels the full force of a tackle from England and British and Irish Lions prop Mako Vunipola

Saracens soaked up further Chiefs bombardment, and eventually struck back with a try of their own just before the hour mark, with American international winger Chris Wyles taking a pass from England lock Maro Itoje to score in the corner after their big forwards had worked their way downfield.

Farrell missed the touchline conversion, so Exeter still had their noses in front at 13-11 entering the closing stages, but then came the dramatic finale.

Saracens drove into Exeter territory, Farrell offloaded to Schalk Brits and his looped pass found Ellery, the early replacement for Ashton. The winger still had plenty to do but he managed to fly over Slade and dot the ball down in the corner.

Farrell missed the touchline conversion, which left Exeter only three points behind and within striking distance, with time fast running out, but the Chiefs kept believing, and there was no better time for Simmonds – who had only been on the pitch for 11 minutes as a replacement for Waldrom – to strike the killer blow than with the clock in the red zone, and no opportunity for Saracens to respond once more.

It completed a perfect week for Simmonds, who only three days earlier had been named Premiership Sevens Player of the Year at a glittering ceremony in London.

It was also a very special occasion for Irish centre Ian Whitten, who led the team out to thunderous noise at the start of the game to mark his 100th appearance for the club.

"It was a big game for Ian," said Baxter. "Henry had got injured in the run-in and as a centre pairing, Ian and Ollie Devoto did what I like players to do, when I talk about players picking a team. They made themselves the centre pairing with some big performances.

Emotional scenes as Sandy Park erupts on the final whistle as Exeter confirm their place in the Aviva Premiership final

"We left Ian out for Harlequins away and picked Campo (Michele Campagnaro), and we felt that was the right thing to do, and I remember him looking at me and I could tell he was thinking: 'Is this an opportunity lost? If we keep winning, I might not play in the big games at the end'.

"But again, it showed how we were prepared to make changes week by week to keep that team fresh and maintain energy levels. If you look at the way Campo played at Quins, it was a really good decision, and it also freed Ian up to come back fighting, really energetic and firing, because his performances in the last couple of games of the regular season made him the natural selection for the semi and final."

Many thought the television pictures of Baxter leaving his seat at the back of the grandstand to walk down and greet his family, soon after Ellery had scored, was a concession by the Exeter supremo that the Premiership dream was over for another year, but that was not the case.

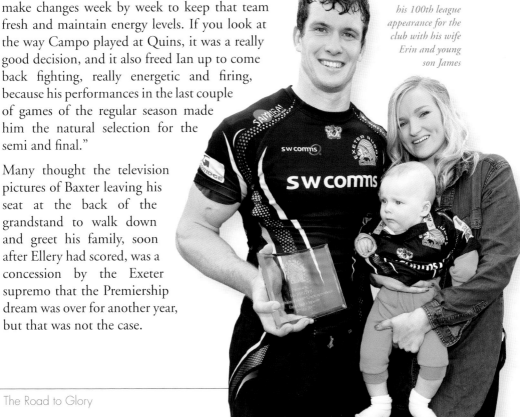

Ian Whitten holds a memento to celebrate his 100th league appearance for the club with his wife Erin and young son James

"I didn't think our chance had gone because we had won so many matches late in the game, but I knew it would be tough to win the match from that point," he recalled.

"Because leaving my seat was on television and it was at that stage of the game, I think a lot of people made the assumption that I thought we had blown it.

"The truth is I walk down from my seat about that time every home game, whether we win or lose. I see my wife and my children on the way past, and my dad and mum, and then I go down and see my gran, so that was all the same as usual.

"I wasn't laughing and joking, because at that stage there were a couple of minutes left in the game and we were behind, so there is a reason why I have got that (stern) look on my face.

"My gran actually said to me 'I am sorry about this', but I replied 'hold on, don't worry, the game is not over yet'.

"I was stood in the middle of the stand because I normally go halfway down, watch the end of the game from there so I can have a good view, and then it gives me an easy shoot down to the pitchside on the final whistle, otherwise I wouldn't get there for five minutes because of the crowd.

"I hadn't done anything different to normal, but what was fantastic was I got to watch a scrum penalty, Sladey's kick and the maul, all from the middle of the grandstand, and have a bit of excitement when the try was scored."

One of my abiding memories of that game will be the sight of Baxter hugging and jumping up and down with a man stood next to him.

I wondered if it was like a moment from the film Notting Hill, where the characters played by Hugh Grant and Julia Roberts finally confirm their relationship in a packed press conference, and 'Bernie', played by Hugh Bonneville, turns to his left and hugs a surprised, but apparently happy, female journalist he has never met before!

But not a bit of it, as Baxter explained.

"It was Andy Bassett, who I used to play with for Exeter, and he sits in the middle of the grandstand. My wife and I, and Andy and his wife, see each other socially and we go out for dinner and we are good friends, and have been since we played rugby together," said Baxter.

"I will see him and his wife for a handshake and a hug most games, but it just so happened we all had the chance to go a bit mad there, and those were some really nice moments."

Baxter said he felt the scenes at the end of the game were probably the most incredible he had ever seen at Sandy Park.

"But as great as it was emotionally, the key for me was how quickly could we move on from it, and I know I moved on from it emotionally very quickly, because I knew we had to, and the other coaches did, and to be fair to the players, they did as well," added Baxter.

"We said to them: 'It was a fantastic game, won in a fantastic way, but people will probably talk more about it being such a good game if we can repeat it in the final', and I think we did manage to park it pretty well and move on very quickly."

Just one match now lay between Exeter and lifting their first Premiership crown.

PREMIERSHIP SEMI-FINAL

EXETER CHIEFS 18 SARACENS 16

(Saturday, May 20, Sandy Park)

Chiefs: P Dollman (H Slade 68); J Nowell, I Whitten, O Devoto (M Campagnaro 70), J Short; G Steenson (capt), S Townsend (W Chudley 54); B Moon (C Rimmer 59), L Cowan-Dickie (J Yeandle 59), H Williams (T Francis 59); D Dennis (M Lees 42-47), G Parling; K Horstmann (M Lees 60), D Armand, T Waldrom (S Simmonds 68).

Saracens: A Goode; C Ashton (M Ellery 11), M Bosch, D Taylor, C Wyles; O Farrell, R Wigglesworth; M Vunipola (T Lamositele 42-47), J George (S Brits 45), V Koch; M Itoje, G Kruis; M Rhodes (S Burger 10), J Wray, B Vunipola. Replacements (not used): P Du Plessis, K Brown, B Spencer, A Lozowski.

Chiefs: Tries – Nowell, S Simmonds; Conversion – Steenson; Penalties – Steenson (2).
Saracens: Tries – Wyles, Ellery; Penalties – Farrell (2).

HT: 6-6. **Referee:** Wayne Barnes (RFU). **Attendance:** 12,436.

Mr Reliable, Gareth Steenson, kicks the winning penalty three minutes from the end of extra time

CHAPTER 11

History Makers

Premiership final
Saturday 27   W   Wasps 20   Exeter Chiefs 23

AS fantastic as it was beating reigning champions Saracens in the semi-final, Exeter Chiefs had won nothing yet.

I am sure the major concern of everyone connected with the club was, given the incredible nature of the win and the amazing post-match scenes and celebrations, how could the players lift themselves one more time to defeat Wasps?

How could you move on from beating Saracens quickly enough?

As mentioned in the last chapter, it was something the Exeter coaching staff had discussed even before the semi-final, such is the meticulous planning that goes into everything on the playing side of the club.

Everyone was on message after the Sarries game – the players, coaches etc – and fly-half Gareth Steenson was quick to state: "The job is not done yet. The final will be another huge encounter for us, and we have to prepare this week and get ourselves ready for it."

Gareth Steenson is enveloped by the big arms of Wasps players Ashley Johnson and Joe Launchbury

Jack Nowell once again shows his ability to score on the big occasion

Jack Nowell celebrates his try at Twickenham with Stuart Townsend and Ian Whitten

However, it is one thing to say all the right things, it is another to do them, especially when everyone around you at Sandy Park is still buzzing with excitement over the semi-final victory.

Lessons learnt early in the campaign, though, were to prove beneficial, as Baxter explained.

"At the start of the season, we hadn't left the season before behind us, and we learnt massive lessons as a coaching team over how to leave things behind, and what we did really well as a team was to leave the semi-final behind.

"I was still getting text messages from people on the Wednesday and Thursday about winning the semi-final, and we had a final at Twickenham on the Saturday, so if I was getting texts and emails, every player would have been as well.

"By the time we had got to the Wednesday, we had enjoyed a couple of good training days and we showed the players a bit of a musical montage of the semi-final, and I said to them: 'Look, these are our last training sessions, I know you will all be getting messages and Wednesday is our media day and those of you doing media will get asked about the semi-final and about how you won it and knocking out Saracens. Everyone will want to talk about the semi-final, even though you have got a final this weekend. As good as it was and as great as it felt, you have got to leave it behind'."

When Baxter and his coaching staff sat down to name their team for the final, one of the biggest decisions they had to make was over the wing position.

However, to anyone who followed the Chiefs closely, the omission of James Short – the club's top try scorer for the season with 14 – not just from the starting XV but the match-day 23, would not have come as too big a surprise, even though it might have appeared a cruel call to many.

I remember having a discussion live on *BBC Radio Devon* with my summariser John Lockyer and studio presenter Alan Richardson around three months before about the great season Short was having, but saying that, if everyone was fit and available and the Chiefs were playing the Premiership final today, he would not even be in the 23.

That was no reflection on how he was performing, as he was a joy to watch throughout the campaign, but I could not see Baxter leaving out either Jack Nowell or Olly Woodburn, and when considering an outside back replacement for the bench, there were other players who offered more versatility to Short than just playing on the wing.

The bad news for Short, who had started and played well in the semi-final against his old club Saracens – from whom he scored a try in their 22-18 Premiership final victory over Leicester at Twickenham in 2011 – was that Woodburn, who missed the last-four clash with a hamstring injury picked up against Gloucester, was fit for the final.

"Shorty had done really well for us and played in a hugely emotional semi-final, but his competition was Jack, a fantastic player who is very important to us and gets us on the front foot, and is under-rated in some of the things he does, an England international and in the British and Irish Lions squad, and on the other wing Olly, the Players' Player of the Year who had enjoyed a great season," explained Baxter.

"It was a tough decision, and a number of people said to me when they saw the selection 'that feels tough, it feels wrong', and it did feel wrong for all kinds of reasons, but the feeling right probably came out on top.

"I can't say James Short didn't deserve to play in the final, because he probably did, but we probably had other players you could say deserved to play in the final.

"It just comes down to what feels right, and who has laid it out on the field the most.

"I think the toughest thing wasn't necessarily leaving him out of the starting line-up, it was not even having him on the bench, and that was a tough call (the Chiefs opted for Italian international centre Michele Campagnaro instead).

"The great thing was he got to travel and warm up and be fully involved in it all, because Olly wasn't quite fit the week before. There was going to be a doubt during the week over whether his hamstring would hold up, so Shorty was training and was fully with the team other than playing.

"He might say differently, and he might feel that was awful and was real torture for him, but from my perspective it was probably a bit better than being completely left out.

"He was very close to being picked, but it wasn't the only tough call we had to make for the semi-final, final or through the course of the season.

"It is now down to him to perform during the next season, to perform to a level that is above the other wingers so that the decision is not close, and that he is the natural choice and that it feels right and proper that he plays, and we have got quite a few guys like that in the squad."

Baxter broke the news to Short in a phone call on the Monday night after the Sarries game. If any changes are made to the team each week, Baxter rings the players who have been dropped to let them know the decision and explain the reasoning behind it, before the team is announced.

"It was pretty tough from my perspective because I knew it would hurt him," admitted Baxter.

"He was very good about it. At the end of the day, players can either make it quite tough for you, or they can take it well and move on, and to be fair to Shorty he took the conversation well and we dealt with it there and then and moved on."

While Baxter had his own difficult selection decisions to make, the Chiefs received a bit of a bonus when the news came out that Wasps would be without the great attacking threat of 60-cap Australian international full-back Kurtley Beale, who had gone off in the semi-final win over Leicester with a hamstring injury.

It meant South African star Willie Le Roux moving to the number 15 shirt, and Josh Bassett coming in on the wing.

"It did mean a very good player was missing for them, but it didn't affect us too much because our approach to the game was that Wasps had a lot of potential match winners, and we needed to take those match winners out of the game as much as possible (by denying them the ball), and that wouldn't change whether Kurtley Beale was playing or not," explained Baxter.

In the Premiership final 12 months before against Saracens, Exeter had paid dearly for a first-half performance where they did not really turn up on the big occasion, and trailed 23-3 after only 37 minutes, leaving them with too big a mountain to climb.

Maybe that was because just reaching the final was a great achievement to many of the players, and winning it would merely have been the icing on the cake.

This time around though, there was a totally different mindset in the camp, and one often referred to by the players and coaches in the closing weeks of the season.

Anything but a win in the final was going to be a major disappointment to them, and they were determined not to make the same mistake again.

"We put a massive amount of focus on the fact we had let ourselves down the year before, and the big lesson for us needed to be how we hit the field, but the truth was everything was better this time because we had experienced little things the year before," explained Baxter.

"We stayed in a hotel the night before which was in a slightly better location (the Brentford Novotel in 2016 and the Heston Hyde Hotel in 2017), so our trip from the hotel to the ground was a little bit better and our timings were a little bit better (the team coach even did a dry run to Twickenham the day before to make sure there were no unforeseen problems likely to arise).

"We built in extra time so we didn't end up getting rushed at all when we arrived at Twickenham, so the guys could turn up and take their time in the changing rooms.

"The ticketing scenario, the players knowing exactly where their wives, girlfriends and family were going to be in the stadium, everyone getting their tickets sorted nice and early… all the little things that can potentially be distractions for you, we knew what they were, where the issues might be, and where they would come from, and we dealt with them all.

"We had obviously turned up at Twickenham the year before and seen an incredible Chiefs crowd welcoming the guys into the stadium, which if that is your first time there and you don't know that is coming, that can be quite overwhelming, in a totally positive way, but you also don't know how it will affect you, so it helps you prepare if you know those things are coming.

"We even had a better room set aside for the players to meet their families after the game and have food, and though that doesn't necessarily affect your performance, everyone knew exactly what was happening, and all of those things helped us very much focus purely on the rugby."

Exeter certainly did learn the lessons of 12 months before in a Twickenham showdown in which Woodburn for Short was their only change from the semi-final, whilst Wasps made three, with former Gloucester scrum-half Dan Robson preferred to Joe Simpson at number nine, and Tommy Taylor taking over from Ashley Johnson at hooker, in addition to the inclusion of Bassett for the injured Beale.

Don Armand, who was named man of the match in the final, rises high to claim line-out ball

It was the most appropriate final, with first against second in the final table, and the Premiership's top two try scorers at the end of the regular season fighting it out, with Wasps on 89 and Exeter on 86 – 20 clear of next-best Saracens.

Conditions could not have been much better as Wasps fly-half Danny Cipriani got the game underway, with very warm sunshine beating down on the Twickenham pitch, mixed with a gentle, cooling breeze, and what followed for the near-80,000 capacity crowd was arguably the best ever Premiership final – fantastic for the neutral, but agony for the supporters of Exeter and Wasps.

It was nip and tuck all the way through the normal 80 minutes, and then 20 minutes of extra time, and it came within a whisker of going to a penalty kicking competition to decide the destiny of the title.

The OPTA statistics for the game were quite amazing, and showed just how much dominance Exeter had at times, particularly in extra time, and how well Wasps did to stay in the contest until the death with some superb defence.

The Chiefs enjoyed 68 per cent of both territory and possession; Wasps made 299 tackles in the 100 minutes – an incredible three a minute – compared to Exeter's 114, and not surprisingly they had 13 of the top 14 tacklers in the game, led by centre Jimmy Gopperth with 22.

The Chiefs made 222 ball carries to Wasps' 135; they made 730 metres with them, compared to 526, yet despite all of that, it took a Steenson penalty a minute from time to take the contest into extra time, and then another successful kick by the Irishman three minutes from the end of that to finally see off Wasps and clinch Exeter's first Premiership crown.

Exeter made their intentions clear right from the off when Steenson boldly turned down a pretty simple penalty chance after only four minutes in favour of kicking to the corner, but they lost possession soon after the line-out and the scoring opportunity was gone.

Steenson then suffered a huge hit from Wasps No.8 Nathan Hughes, which saw the Chiefs cough up the ball, but Cipriani kicked wastefully direct into touch when he had a three-on-two overlap outside him.

Exeter broke the deadlock in the 14th minute with a try straight off the training ground, with two of their England youngsters combining to great effect.

The Chiefs kicked another penalty to touch to secure a line-out close to the 22-metre line, Dave Dennis won the ball and fed Thomas Waldrom, who popped up a pass to Cowan-Dickie, and his wonderful sleight of hand provided an inside ball for winger Nowell, who produced a clinical finish to repeat his try-scoring feat in the final the year before.

The *Twitter* banter between the two friends in the days following the game was priceless, with Cowan-Dickie humorously suggesting that fellow Cornishman Nowell had not been grateful enough to him for his score!

It was a very clever ploy by Exeter, who had caused Wasps a lot of problems with their driving maul in the past few seasons. With Wasps committing resources to defending the drive, the Chiefs moved the ball quickly away from the maul, and worked a lovely move that found their opponents short on numbers around the fringes.

"Great credit to Ali Hepher and Rob Hunter, they actually spend a lot of time looking at where these opportunities might come," said Baxter. "You look at a lot of line-outs and you look at a lot of defensive set-ups to see if you feel you can drag that bit of space out.

"Although we have run that play, or similar elements of that play before, we have got to win the line-out first before we even run any of the plays, then Stu Townsend's dummy around the front is perfectly timed and just holds their defence enough, then there is Luke's carry and pass, and the angle and timing of Jack's run. There is a lot to get right there, and you don't have that many opportunities to run that.

"It shows great quality by the coaching staff to pick that out, and great quality to walk through, jog through, and run through it enough times in training to nail it with that precision in the match."

Baxter added: "Jack had some really big moments in the game, including that try, but there was a period of the match when he tried to force things a little bit too much, because he threw a couple of offloads he didn't need to throw, and he maybe tried a little bit too hard to do it himself.

"What was nice was that, as a team, we managed to remember the lessons of the season and reined that back a little bit.

"You have got to make passes and you have got to do things when it is on, but you don't have to do more than everybody else on the field, you have just got to do your job really well, and I think we managed to keep doing that a little bit more for a little bit longer than Wasps did, and that eventually created that pressure scenario where we won the game."

Steenson converted sublimely from the touchline and Exeter led 7-0.

Wasps responded with a simple Gopperth penalty four minutes later after Ian Whitten had strayed offside in midfield, but just before the half-hour mark, Exeter grabbed their second try.

Exeter club captain Jack Yeandle celebrates winning the Premiership with Dave Dennis on the final whistle

Phil Dollman is rolled onto his back by Christian Wade but is about to get the ball down for Exeter's second try

Phil Dollman ignores his crutches to celebrate Exeter's Premiership win, after limping off in the final

Working a move off the platform of a solid scrum on Wasps' 22, Ollie Devoto straightened the line with a powerful run, and managed to offload out the back of his hand to full-back Phil Dollman, who celebrated his call-up to the Wales squad only days before with his first try of the season.

The touchdown was again converted by Steenson to make it 14-3 and Exeter were firmly in the driving seat, but Wasps left the Chiefs in no doubt that they still had a major game on their hands.

Only great work by Whitten prevented Bassett from scoring in the corner, while Hughes was also thwarted in his attempts to get to the whitewash.

Then, right on the stroke of half-time, an attack up the middle saw great hands by Cipriani, Taylor and Robson put Gopperth in for a try beside the posts, which he converted himself with the last kick of the half, to leave the Chiefs only leading 14-10 at the break.

Gopperth always seems to have brilliant games against the Chiefs, and this occasion was to be no different.

That was a blow to Exeter right on half-time, and Wasps continued their onslaught at the start of the second period, with suddenly the momentum of the game all with them.

Man-mountain Hughes broke two or three tackles to take possession up to halfway, and when Christian Wade kicked the ball deep into Exeter territory, Woodburn slipped momentarily in the chase and a favourable bounce allowed England's Elliot Daly to gather and leap over the stricken Chiefs player to grab a try.

Gopperth's conversion went in off an upright to put Wasps ahead at 17-14 for the first time in the game.

Hughes was a thorn in Exeter's side all afternoon and the England back rower had an immense game, although he did give the penalty away right at the end of normal time that saw Steenson level the scores at 20-20 by handling the ball off his feet at a ruck.

However, he was more than matched by his opposite number, Thomas Waldrom, who was trying to make up for missing the previous year's final through injury.

Thomas Waldrom makes one of his record-breaking 37 carries in the Premiership final as he runs at the heart of the Wasps defence

He racked up a scarcely believable 37 carries, the highest ever registered by OPTA since they started recording the statistic nearly a decade before. He also made 106 metres with ball in hand.

"I think it was one of Nathan's best games against us," said Baxter. "We normally manage to handle him pretty well, and I thought he showed that he is still a developing player, and a very important player for Wasps.

"But overall, if you look at his contribution compared to that of Thomas Waldrom, I think Tom came out on top, if you look at the number of ball carries that he made, the number of real, tough, hard metres that he made, and how prepared he was to just get off the floor and carry again and give us another target.

"You have got to say that someone who is prepared to carry 37 times in a match and is so willing to keep standing there and doing it and being in the thick of it, is a guy who is massively driven to win a game of rugby. Hughes was great, but I thought Tommy was fantastic."

Despite Waldrom's efforts though, the Premiership man of the match award actually went to Don Armand, who was subsequently selected for England's summer tour to Argentina, where he was joined by clubmates Devoto, Jack Maunder, Harry Williams and Henry Slade.

Dollman limped out of the fray in the 46th minute, and seeing him go up to collect his winners' medal at the end on crutches, no doubt knowing deep down that his chance to win his first Welsh cap had gone, was the one big downside of the whole afternoon for the Chiefs.

It was so cruel, given the fact it had taken such a lengthy time for him to get his first international call-up, at the age of 32, when he had deserved a cap for so long. I actually wrote the day before the game that it would be just typical of his luck to get injured in the final and miss out, and sadly so it proved.

"It was tough for Dolly, and I heard a couple of people say to him after the game whether he would have preferred to win a Wales cap or be a Premiership winner, and he said 'winning the final every day of the week'," said Baxter.

"In a weird way, getting injured was even tougher for him, because you kind of wonder if he had toured with Wales and played really well in one of their games, whether he would have ended up with the Lions, the way they pulled several Welsh players across to their squad.

"Phil wouldn't change what happened for the world though. He has been a great club guy, he has been with us a long time, and he was the first player I signed on my own as head coach, and to go from being part of our Championship-winning team to playing in a Premiership final and scoring a try is incredible.

"I do feel for him, and I know he was desperate to go on the Wales tour and it would have been a real highlight of his career, but hopefully there will be more highlights to come for him, and hopefully with us over the next year or two."

Matters continued to go against Exeter, as Dollman's replacement Slade got too much on a penalty kick to touch very similar to the one he had produced with such precision in the semi-final against Saracens to set up the match-winning try, and the Chiefs lost valuable ground.

Baxter brought on four fresh forwards – a new front row of Carl Rimmer, Jack Yeandle and Tomas Francis, and Mitch Lees in the second row – only for a Gopperth penalty soon after to extend Wasps' lead to six points, but Exeter kept believing.

"Our game plan was largely very good," said Baxter. "There was a period when we started to waver from it, where we fed Wasps a couple pieces of possession.

"Their tries either side of half-time could have hurt a lot of teams but we knew how we had conceded them, and we managed to deal with that scenario.

"When you see how the whole of the rest of the game went, once Wasps took the lead, there was a huge show of character from us but also a real show of how we needed to win the game.

"We started to run exits, we put multi-phases together, we denied them the ball, and we did very little to feed them possession in danger areas."

Steenson kicked a lengthy penalty ten minutes later to reduce the deficit to 20-17 after Wasps were penalised for going in at the side after a great carry by Geoff Parling, who claimed 11 line-outs during the game.

However, when Exeter were awarded another simple kick almost in front of the posts with 11 minutes remaining when Le Roux was caught offside, they amazingly went for the scrum from the penalty.

It looked like it was going to be a Chris Robshaw moment – he famously turned down a penalty against Wales in the World Cup which could have earned England a draw, in favour of going for the victory, and which eventually saw them eliminated from the tournament, as the decision failed to produce Exeter the try they were looking for.

There was a lengthy injury stoppage before the Chiefs had to give their decision to referee JP Doyle over what they wanted to do – plenty of time to get a message on from the sidelines – but nothing was forthcoming.

Interestingly, listening back to the *BT Sport* commentary after the game, the pundits were somewhat split over what to do.

"We didn't send a message on of what we wanted," revealed Baxter. "We said we would leave it to the players.

"The reason we didn't want to kick the goal and instead went for the scrum was that our game plan was based significantly on denying Wasps the ball and being prepared to go to the corners and take them on with our pack of forwards.

"Did it feel a bit weird at the time? Potentially, but if we had kicked the penalty there would still have been 10 minutes left to play, we would have got the ball back in our own half from the restart, and then we had to be prepared to either play out of our half, or kick the ball away, or make a mistake, which would have given Wasps possession, and our whole game plan was about denying them field position and possession, so on that basis the decision felt okay."

That was also the reason why the Chiefs, puzzlingly at the time, resisted the temptation to go for a drop goal towards the end of the normal 80 minutes and extra time, despite their supporters crying out for them to do so.

"Ultimately, sticking to that mantra won us the game," added Baxter.

"When we didn't score off the scrum, it felt a bit weird, but I didn't think it would be a defining moment of the game, even if we had taken the shot at goal and kicked it."

There was also the possibility that Wasps could have gone to uncontested scrums, with Marty Moore joining fellow tight-head prop Phil Swainston off the field with an injury, but director of rugby Dai Young put loose-head prop Matt Mullan back on to avoid that scenario.

"It wasn't as simple as saying it would be a big advantage to Wasps if it had gone to uncontested scrums, because they would have had to take another player off, so they would have been down to 14 men," explained Baxter.

"Could it have been manipulated in the last couple of minutes, when we were five metres out, and it goes to uncontested scrums and we can't scrummage? That could have happened, but fair play to Wasps, they never tried to do that and that is great credit to Dai."

With time appearing to be running out for Exeter, Hughes suddenly infringed at the ruck, and the Chiefs had one last chance to level matters, and up stepped Steenson, as cool as a cucumber, to slot the 30-metre kick, level the scores at 20-20 and send the game into extra time, as had remarkably happened the last time JP Doyle had refereed the final, in 2014, when Northampton beat Saracens 24-20 with a last-minute try by Alex Waller.

That kick was a huge psychological blow to Wasps, and looking around at the two sets of players as they waited to start extra time, I could only see there being one winner, and that was Exeter.

The Chiefs' body language was better, in my opinion, and they looked fitter, and Baxter was also confident at that stage.

"Once we got to extra time, I genuinely think we looked the more comfortable team, and looked like we knew how we were going to win," he said.

"The bench always play a big part and we had rotated the side a bit in the lead-up to the final so they all had plenty of game time under their belts, and they were all fully involved in the process of how we wanted to play and how we wanted to do things, and that worked fantastically well for us.

"If you play the way we did during the season, by having all those extra minutes of ball-in-play time week by week, extra time becomes less of a challenge for you than it is for another side."

He added: "The only period in extra time when we were under a little bit of pressure, Don Armand got harshly penalised at a line-out, when he jumped and hooked his hand around the ball and pulled it down, but he got penalised for taking a player in the air.

"That gave Wasps field position from a very good kick into our corner, but we weathered the storm there, and that was almost the only bit of field position they got in the whole 20 minutes of extra time.

"There was just one moment at the start of the second half of it, when they kicked off, and we were a little bit fortunate because Henry Slade had the ball stripped from him, but we got the line-out, and we were never out of the Wasps half after that for the whole of the ten-minute period, until we scored and they restarted the game and we saw the clock out."

The Chiefs could have possibly wrapped the game up five minutes before the end of extra time, when semi-final hero Sam Simmonds – who had come on as a 60th-minute replacement for Dennis – looked like he had completed an amazing double by burrowing his way over at a ruck.

One camera angle suggested the ball had been grounded over the line, but after looking at the video evidence numerous times, with the tension around Twickenham rising each time the incident was played back on the big screen, Doyle and television match official Rowan Kitt felt the footage was inconclusive and the try was ruled out.

"When you look at it several times, there does look like a grounding, but what we did really well was get on with it after the decision had been made," said Baxter.

"It was another really good example of the lessons we had learned through the season. Things aren't always going to go your way, you are not going to go through a whole

Exeter players join their supporters in 'The Tomahawk Chop' as it rings out around Twickenham

game without making a mistake, at times you are going to be under pressure, and at some stage you might be behind in a game, but it is important to refocus very quickly.

"We did that, we went through some scrums, and we made some good decisions. A scrum collapsed and you don't have to play the ball away from that, even if a referee asks you to. You only have to do that from a stood-up scrum.

"Tom Waldrom and Will Chudley decided not to play the ball away, so it would be another scrum, and we kept working hard and following our processes, and we won the penalty."

It was given for Wasps prop Mullan taking the scrum to the floor, and it gave Steenson yet another huge pressure 25-metre kick, this time to almost certainly win the game and cement his place in Exeter's history.

He had not missed a kick all afternoon, and just like his successful effort at the end of normal time, the outcome was never in doubt as he bisected the posts and the wonderful 'Tomahawk Chop', so synonymous with the Chiefs, started to reverberate once again around Twickenham.

You could not have wished for a better person or player to be standing over the ball in those sorts of situations. So many times in the past, Steenson had slotted crucial kicks on his way to amassing more than 2,000 points for the club, and you would have put your mortgage on him doing so again.

It was also very fitting in the year where the club had granted him a testimonial for his ten years of service to the Chiefs.

"I have watched the kicks back a few times now, and they never look like missing. They are absolutely through the middle," said Baxter.

"It shows fantastic qualities, bottle, whatever you want to call it, and they were great examples of the kind of player Gareth has become.

"I hope they are key kicks in him continuing to move that way as a player.

"I love the fact that he might get the opportunity to do those in some really big European games, or more big Premiership games, and Gareth is likely to use those kicks as a driver to say: 'I can perform at this level, and can do so because of the way that I practice, and the way I prepare mentally.

"Those are things he now needs to drive and for them to continue to be in his game, but also things we would like to think he will potentially pass on to the young fly-halves coming through the club as well."

If Steenson had missed, or the penalty opportunity had not come along, the match would have gone to a kicking competition for the first time in Premiership history, though it did happen once in a Heineken Cup semi-final between Cardiff Blues and Leicester Tigers in May 2009.

It would have been a very interesting situation, as each team would have had to pick three kickers, to take two kicks apiece from different positions on the pitch.

Wasps still had recognised goalkickers Gopperth, Cipriani and Daly on the field, and Exeter had Steenson and Slade, but who would have been number three, with Devoto having already been replaced?

"We were still debating it!" confessed Baxter. "We had a couple of candidates in mind, but it may well have been Chudders (Will Chudley) we would have asked to have a go from in front of the posts.

"But once we got that bit of field position towards the end, all our debating on the kickers stopped, because there was a momentum in the game that felt like we were going to force something to happen."

It must have been an incredible feeling for Baxter when the final whistle went, having lost at Twickenham on six previous visits as both a player and coach, with those four National Trophy final defeats and the 2016 Premiership final against Saracens added to by the 22-6 league loss to Harlequins in 'Big Game Six' in December 2013.

He was pictured sharing an emotional moment with his wife Jo and children Jack and Annie beside the tunnel soon after the game had finished, and shedding the odd tear.

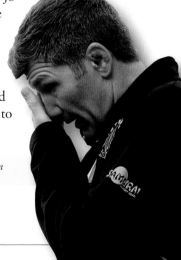

Baxter admitted it was very hard to put into words exactly how he felt when the whistle went.

"To be honest all I really wanted to do was see the family, and make sure they were okay because it obviously meant a lot to them as well," admitted Baxter.

Exeter head coach Rob Baxter fights back the tears after spending an emotional moment on the touchline with his family

"You never really know how you are going to feel until it happens. It felt a bit funny, but whatever anybody said, we were the champions of England.

"It just felt like a really nice reward for a lot of hard work over a long period of time by a lot of people, and it just felt really great that so many people could say: 'I was a part of that', especially for those who genuinely were a part of it, who contributed well and helped move the club forward.

"That included a lot of people who I call my friends, my colleagues, or people I work with really closely. The squad of players who did it were right at the forefront of it, but also people involved before and not involved now.

"There were a lot of emotions tied up with it for me. I didn't want to run around whooping and hollering, but it felt nice to be shaking people's hands and having a hug and smiling.

"It felt nice just to be smiling, and to see the boys go up there on the podium and get the trophy."

It would have meant more to Baxter than maybe anyone else at the club because of the proud history his family enjoys with the Chiefs, going back through several decades, with father John, younger brother Richie and uncle Paul, like him, having also played for Exeter.

"That is what made it all feel amazing in a very broad way, because there had been such a long burn to get to that point," explained Baxter.

"It sounds really odd to say it, but there wasn't an explosion of joy for me. It was a bit of relief, a bit of 'job done', but also real satisfaction over the reward it had given a lot of people.

"The hard part of the job is when you let good players and good people go, or you don't pick good players and good people, and you do quite a lot of things that are quite tough.

"The real positive every week is when you select your team, but every week you phone the people who you know are going to be disappointed. You don't phone the people who you have selected, so you don't often get the good side of it.

"It means you feel for a lot of people as well, so when you actually win something, you feel justification for a lot of the decisions that have been made."

Baxter has always been excellent at keeping things on an even keel, whether the team is winning or losing.

The words of Rudyard Kipling's 'If' inscribed above the door leading out onto Centre Court at Wimbledon sums up his approach very nicely.

'If you can meet with Triumph and Disaster, and treat those two imposters just the same....'

However, I must admit I was genuinely quite shocked at his demeanour when he went into the bowels of Twickenham Stadium to conduct his after-match press conference in front of the national print media.

There were no smiles. His facial expression was much the same as it had been speaking after the Saracens defeat 12 months before, and it looked like the last place in the world that he wanted to be at that moment – which was very unusual for someone usually so comfortable in front of such a gathering and who realises that dealing with the media is an important part of the job.

He asked the press to fire their questions first at skipper Steenson, who was alongside him, so the happy Irishman could shoot off and get showered, before giving a proper answer to every question asked of him, and then heading for the exit.

"I genuinely couldn't wait to get home," admitted Baxter.

"In a weird way, the emotions after the game were in some ways harder to deal with than the year before, when we had lost.

"In my time at the club as head coach, there have been a lot of games when I have stood in changing rooms, including the final the year before, and said: 'We can learn from this loss and move forward', and then to actually sit on the bus on the way home and think that we had achieved something was an interesting emotion to have.

"For the first couple of days after Twickenham, I was trying to get my head around what the approach for the next season would be, based on the fact we had won, and what we wanted to achieve now and what we were going to talk about, and that was an interesting challenge for me.

"I didn't hang around at the club for long when we got back to Sandy Park after the game. I stayed for about 20 minutes or half an hour and I then went home with my family.

"I genuinely didn't really feel like having a massive party and getting drunk, and actually forgetting about what a fantastic day it was, so we went home and I sat in the garden with my wife until about half past two in the morning, and we had a couple of quiet drinks and listened to some music, and we just sat there with the patio heater on and just chilled and just talked about the day, and it was really nice to do that, rather than go mad.

"It didn't feel like a day to go mad to me. It just felt like a day to sit back and relish it and enjoy it, and spend a bit of time on our own, and have a bit of quiet time."

After a couple of days of letting what he and the club had achieved sink in, Baxter admitted he savoured the victory parade through the streets of Exeter, when thousands of Chiefs fans came out to join in the celebrations and cheer on their heroes.

"I really enjoyed the parade, way more than I did the LV= Cup parade, because by then I'd relaxed enough and cleared things up in my own head about where we wanted to go and what we wanted to do, and what winning the final had meant, and it was great to have a couple of pints of beer, and look at the crowd and just be back with the players and the staff," he said.

"My son had just left university and around 10 of his mates from there were coming round to our house on Tuesday afternoon and evening for a barbecue, so on the Monday I asked Tony Rowe if I could take the trophy home with me.

The Exeter players receive a tremendous welcome from their supporters on arrival at Twickenham Stadium

"I had some pictures on the Monday night taken of me and my wife having a cup of tea sat next to the trophy, and the following day my son and his mates came round – and we hadn't told him beforehand – but sat on the table in the middle of the garden was the Aviva Premiership trophy, and that was nice to be able to do that.

"Those are special personal moments that you can really savour."

Winning the Premiership for the first time in the club's history was incredibly special, but doing it in such style by setting Premiership records on the way for most bonus-point wins and surpassing some of the great Premiership teams of the past decade or so, surely made it even more satisfying?

"I maybe might have said 'yes' straight after the final and agreed that it was a great way to do it, but this shows how players influence you," explained Baxter.

"We had some individual meetings when we returned for pre-season, and one player – who I will not name – when I asked him what his individual driver would be for the new season and what his thoughts were going forward, he said: 'I would like to be part of a Premiership-winning team in a more dominant way'.

"I was initially taken aback by that, but when I thought about it I kind of got what he meant, because we didn't go out there from game one last season and say 'this is about Exeter'.

"He wants to go out there and be a number one player in the Exeter team, and say this is what we can achieve, and this is how good we are going to be from day one, and be that good every day, and when we get to the final, no-one will doubt we are going to win it, because people will have seen that in us all season.

"I actually like that, and in hindsight, if someone asked me now whether it was great to win the Premiership in the manner that we did, I would say that it was just great to do it, and I'm not actually that bothered how we did it.

"There are nicer ways to win it than banging over a kick with two-and-a-half minutes left, like scoring plenty of tries in the first half an hour and the rest of the game is a procession!

"What was nice was to win it based on our start to the season, because it showed the turnaround that can happen when a group of guys are in it together and decide what they want to do and the fantastic drivers they can have.

"And to do it after losing the final the previous year, to show that wasn't the high point of what Exeter Chiefs were going to be about, made it even more satisfying."

FINAL – WASPS 20 EXETER CHIEFS 23
(Saturday, May 27, Twickenham Stadium)

Wasps: W Le Roux, C Wade, E Daly, J Gopperth, J Bassett; D Cipriani, D Robson (J Simpson 58); M Mullan (S McIntyre 58), T Taylor (A Johnson 64), P Swainston (M Moore 27, M Mullan 83); J Launchbury (capt), M Symons (K Myall 58); J Haskell, T Young (G Thompson 64), N Hughes (G Thompson 18-26). Replacements (not used): A Leiua, F Halai.

Chiefs: P Dollman (H Slade 46); J Nowell, I Whitten, O Devoto (M Campagnaro 74), O Woodburn; G Steenson (capt), S Townsend (W Chudley 50); B Moon (C Rimmer 50), L Cowan-Dickie (J Yeandle 50), H Williams (T Francis 50); D Dennis (S Simmonds 60), G Parling; K Horstmann (M Lees 53), D Armand, T Waldrom.

Wasps: Tries – Gopperth, Daly; Conversions – Gopperth (2); Penalties – Gopperth (2).
Chiefs: Tries – Nowell, Dollman; Conversions – Steenson (2); Penalties – Steenson (3).

HT: 10-14. **Referee:** JP Doyle (RFU). **Attendance:** 79,657.

The Exeter Chiefs backroom staff celebrate their success in the Twickenham changing rooms

Exeter chairman and chief executive Tony Rowe OBE with Lord Mayor of Exeter, Councillor Lesley Robson, and the club mascot Big Chief, at the open-top bus parade to celebrate the Chiefs' title success

CHAPTER 12

Dreams Can Come True

TONY Rowe OBE believes Exeter Chiefs are "writing rugby history" after winning the Premiership title in only their seventh year in the top flight.

They broke two league records in doing so, registering eight successive bonus-point wins, and getting a try-scoring bonus point in nine consecutive games.

They also tied Leicester's proud all-time record, set between 1999 and 2000, of going 17 Premiership matches unbeaten.

Now they have set themselves the target of winning the European Champions Cup.

"I had a meeting with most of the other Premiership chairmen, and I wouldn't say they are envious of us, but they all say we are rewriting the books, and they are asking 'how do you do it?'" said Exeter chairman and chief executive Rowe.

"The Premiership was really a closed shop when we first went in there seven years ago. They wouldn't tell us anything before we went in and how much money we would or wouldn't get. It was a case of 'you will be around here for a season and then you will be gone', but we have rewritten the books."

Rowe admitted the attitude of other Premiership clubs when Chiefs first moved up into the league, and the desire to prove them wrong, had been a real driving force.

He first got involved in Exeter in 1993, when he was asked to put some money in to help them because they were struggling financially.

He eventually took over the running of the club in 1998 and turned it into a limited company so it could become a proper business, and it was not long before he was drawing up a vision of an exciting future, that involved moving to a new ground and playing in the top tier of English rugby.

"I have got involved with lots of things over the years since I have left school, and I am not a person who will take 'no' for an answer, and who will just give something a little go and then run away," explained Rowe, a former Royal Marine, marine engineer and semi-professional powerboat racer who went on to establish a very successful telecommunications business, South West Telecoms, now renamed SW Comms, of which he is still chairman and chief executive.

"If I think something is achievable, I will give it a good old go. Sometimes in my life I have failed, but more often than not it has worked out.

The brains behind Exeter's on-field success, the coaching team of (from left to right) Ricky Pellow, Rob Hunter, Rob Baxter and Ali Hepher

"I always believed that we could get into the Premiership. Why would I build Sandy Park if I didn't think that?

"What a lot of people didn't see is that, behind the scenes, we prepared everything. When we moved from the County Ground to Sandy Park, we were going into an environment which had been designed around the Minimum Standards Criteria for Premiership Rugby, so it ticked all the boxes, but we also showed our ambition with the appointment of Pete Drewett as a full-time director of rugby."

The real masterstroke, though, when Drewett did not bring the success the club craved, was choosing the inexperienced Rob Baxter as head coach, and winning the Premiership was further justification, not that it was needed, of that decision Rowe had taken eight years before.

However, it was not an appointment that was universally praised at the time.

Having moved to a new £15 million stadium at Sandy Park in 2006 and gone full-time, with the intention of getting out of the Championship and into the Premiership, Exeter were just falling short of their goal.

After losing a National Trophy semi-final at Moseley, with the defeat also severely denting their chances of getting promoted as it doubled up as a league game, Rowe decided to dispense with the services of Drewett in March 2009.

Baxter, who had been coaching the forwards at Chiefs, was asked to take over as acting head coach, but two months later he was appointed full-time.

Some supporters believed Rowe was starting to lose interest in the project after the lack of success and accused him of going for the 'cheap option' by selecting the inexperienced Baxter, but that could not be further from the truth.

"What people failed to see was that Rob came back to Exeter Rugby Club after one year at Gloucester the same year that I got involved with the club in 1993," explained Rowe.

"I get on well with the Baxter family and it was Rob's dad, John, who got me involved in the first place, so I had been with Rob and working alongside him for a long time.

"When I brought Ian Bremner in as director of rugby in 1998, Rob took over as team captain from Andy Maunder and I had a working relationship with him.

"When I had to let Bremner go, I phoned Rob and asked him to stand in, with Bob Staddon there as support, and he just took it in his stride.

"I then appointed Pete, and when I let him go, I called on Rob again just to get us through until the end of the season, but the more I thought about it, the more I was saying to myself: 'Why should I look anywhere else for a permanent replacement?'

"I called a special meeting of the board of directors and they were split, and I had to use my casting vote to give him the job.

"I have still got two directors on the board that didn't vote for him, and I remind them of that fact, tongue in cheek, every now and then!

"I said to the board at the time: 'If I am wrong, what have we really lost? A couple of seasons? But we are in no hurry'.

"I have always said to people, 'we will win the Premiership but we are in no hurry, we will win the Champions Cup but we are in no hurry'.

"Rob repaid that faith I had in him very quickly, though I didn't expect him to achieve promotion to the Premiership as fast as he did, at the end of his first full season in charge.

"When we got into the Premiership, it wasn't a shock to us, and Rob took it quite calmly, though deep down he probably thought, how are we going to do this?!

"He stepped up to the challenge, but beyond that, because he is a talented man, he was able to get far more out of the squad we had than anybody ever believed."

The relationship between Rowe and Baxter works very well, and it is an important factor behind the club's success.

"Rob and I only talk when we need to. I am not one of these people that wants a meeting every Monday morning to sit down and analyse what has gone right or wrong," said Rowe.

One anecdote sums it up very well.

"I go into the changing rooms after every game, win or lose, and he told me off three or four seasons ago," explained Rowe.

"Trying to get down to the dressing room from where I am sat at some of the away games is very difficult, and sometimes I would make the effort and other times I wouldn't, and in hindsight, it was based on the result.

Exeter chairman and chief executive Tony Rowe OBE with his wife Sharon and son Morgan at Twickenham

"Rob said to me one day, 'the boys like to see you there, I like to see you there, but you have got to be there every time, win or lose', and I do that now, and it is great because you go through the excitement and pleasure of winning with the players, and sometimes the disappointment of not doing as well as they could have done."

Rowe believes another reason for the club's success is its "close family" feel, which was demonstrated by the way people rallied around to help them get tickets out in time for their home semi-final clash with Saracens.

"It is a close family, and that's what it is about," he said. "Rob controls his bit of the family, I control my bit off the pitch, but they work very much together.

"An example of that was how we reacted to the problems we had with the company issuing our tickets for the semi-final and we ended up having to do it all by hand. The girls worked 12 hours a day for 12 days, and the players knew that and appreciated that, but the girls only did that because they are part of the team. It is not a job of work for them."

Rowe says he has always looked at Leicester, and more recently Saracens, as two rival Premiership clubs who show the way to do things if you want to be successful.

"We have got the greatest respect for the other teams in the Premiership because we are the new boys, and in all the years I have been running the club, since 1998, I have always held up Leicester as a benchmark club, and I have always strived to make sure our club is as good as Leicester, if not better.

"Saracens are also the benchmark for everyone, and Nigel Wray (chairman) and Mark McCall (director of rugby) have done what we are trying to do.

"I first visited Saracens seven seasons ago and I was quite impressed with them. They were building this culture and they knew they had young lads in their Academy like Maro Itoje coming through, and these last two seasons they have been totally formidable.

Exeter Chiefs board members Alan Quantick (finance director, far right) and Keiron Northcott (deputy chief executive), with Keiron's wife Jill, in celebratory mood at Twickenham

"If you try and analyse what Saracens have achieved, they never did it overnight and they just built it up and built it up over many years, and that is what we are doing, and Rob is doing."

The pictures of a delighted Rowe as he celebrated with his son, Morgan, and his special guest for the afternoon, Exeter City chairman Julian Tagg, on the final whistle at Twickenham said all you needed to know about what winning the Premiership title meant to him.

But did he expect the Chiefs to triumph at the end of a season that had started so badly, with only two wins in their opening seven league games?

"We were disappointed to lose at Twickenham the season before, but I think in a way we accepted it because it was Saracens. They are beatable but they are the benchmark. If you beat them then you can actually get to where you are aiming to get to," he explained.

"Did I expect us to win at Twickenham in 2016? I don't think I did if I am brutally honest with myself, but there was a chance we could do it. As it turned out, we had stage fright in the first half of that game and we didn't turn up.

"Coming into the 2016-17 season, I think I might have casually said to Rob that I would be telling the press we were aiming for top six, but he lets the players set their own goals, and they decided they wanted to go for top four again.

"Commercially, I said top six because I don't want to kid people that we are running around with our heads in the clouds. It is such a competitive league and that is borne out by the fact we had to go to the 22nd round of fixtures this past season before the top eight knew exactly in which position they were going to finish.

"It is a really, really tough division to be in, but we got it wrong at the start. I did talk to Rob a few weeks into the season because we were just not right, and he said:

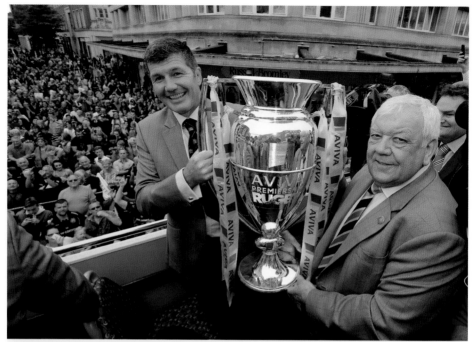

Exeter head coach Rob Baxter and Chiefs chairman and chief executive Tony Rowe OBE hold aloft the Premiership trophy on the open-top bus parade through the streets of Exeter

'I think we got it wrong. We never grounded the guys. They came back from Twickenham and went into the season still thinking they had done really well to be runners-up to the European champions.

"We have a big sales team at SW Comms, and when I used to run it, I would tell them that you could be the best salesperson in the world last month, but on the first day of the next month you started again and had a big, fat zero on your sales sheet. Similarly, that is what you have got to tell the players, but again we learn, and I am quite happy to learn as we go along.

"It hurts Rob sometimes when he gets things wrong, and it is a bit of inexperience that has caused him a couple of headaches, but you have got to accept that, because the upside far, far outweighs the downside of his inexperience.

"There is not much he hasn't experienced now, and he knows after this season what he can get from the guys."

Rowe believes the 13-13 draw at Saracens in early January played a big part in the Chiefs' semi-final success over the reigning champions, and their ultimate triumph at Twickenham.

"I think the guys took a lot of encouragement from that game. For the last two years Saracens have been totally formidable, but when we played them up there in the league early in the New Year, we nearly beat them and we should have done, and the guys knew that when they came off the pitch, and they were angry with themselves that they had let them back into the game."

He was also planning in his head, as the campaign started drawing to a close, what he thought would be the best route Exeter could take to give themselves the greatest chance of winning the title, as shown by a conversation he recalls with television pundit and former Bath and England prop David Flatman.

"I spoke to David around two months before the end of the season, and told him that I fancied Saracens at home and Wasps away at Twickenham, and he agreed with me that he thought we stood a better chance of winning the title by doing it that way, and it was quite strange how it panned out that way," explained Rowe.

The Chiefs chairman also maintained his belief during the semi-final at Sandy Park, even after Mike Ellery had put Saracens 16-13 in front with only five minutes remaining with a try in the corner.

"I never gave up on that game. I just thought we could do it," he said. "The guys had total and utter belief in themselves, and in what the coaches had told them. It is one thing Rob (Baxter) and Ali (Hepher) saying it is a game of attrition and we have got to play our game and keep the momentum and we will wear other teams out because we are fitter than them, but the guys have got to believe that."

The Chiefs were also determined not to have their plans upset by cup competitions, as had happened to them in the 2013-14 season.

"In 2014 we derailed ourselves in the Premiership because we won the LV= Cup. The players had done really well, but to then try and get them focused back on the main game, which was the Premiership, was a really difficult job, and we slipped to eighth that season," said Rowe.

"I said to Rob after that season that, because we are a members club and I have to return a profit each season, we earn our money out of the Aviva Premiership games. Those are the ones that people are going to pay a lot of money to come and watch, so it is important you really focus on that, and don't get sidetracked by cup games.

"Rob will tell you that we didn't fully commit to cup games during the past season, because he was a bit concerned the guys would get too focused on them."

The outcome of the season all came down to 100 minutes at Twickenham, and that Gareth Steenson kick three minutes from the end of extra time to win the match.

"It did take me back to the Ignacio Mieres kick we had in the last play of the game away to Leinster in our first year in the Heineken Cup in 2012, which would have drawn us the game, but he missed it and we lost 9-6," admitted Rowe.

"Inwardly, I knew Steeno could do it, he is rock solid, and when the kick went over it was fantastic, and then it was just a case of hanging on for a couple of minutes.

"What an outstanding player he is. He has been with us for 10 years and that's why we have given him a testimonial year.

"In his early days with us, he was falling off tackles and he wouldn't tackle so much, but he has improved as a player and he is now playing some of the best rugby of his career."

Exeter chairman and chief executive Tony Rowe OBE with Thomas Waldrom in the Twickenham dressing room

Exeter Chiefs

If winning the Premiership title was not brilliant enough in its own right, Rowe admitted that to do it in such fine style, by breaking records for bonus-point wins, made it even more satisfying.

"We had an issue a year or two ago where we couldn't quite put clubs to the sword, and we missed out to Saracens and a top-four place on points difference in 2015," said Rowe.

"Rob instilled in the guys that it is about points, and points make prizes, and you have got to put sides to the sword. The guys got past the Clermont game, which was our turning point, and started to believe in themselves, and started to do what the coaches wanted them to do and were enjoying winning with a bonus point.

"It is not easy to get five-point wins in the Premiership, and to do that game after game was tremendous."

One feature of Exeter's successful season was the response it was greeted with by supporters of rival clubs, with fans' messageboards full of congratulatory comments after the win over Wasps.

That had also been the case throughout the second half of the campaign, each time the Chiefs brought down one of the more fancied runners. They were most definitely everyone's favourite team after the club they supported.

"I think every chairman in the Premiership sent me a text or e-mail to congratulate us, which was lovely, but how long is that going to go on for?" laughed Rowe.

"We were probably everybody's second favourite team because nobody thought we could actually do it, but now we've done it…. and we are going to come back this year and have another go, and the year after…. we are there to be shot at."

He added: "We have got a pride in ourselves and what we do, and what's lovely is it is a West Country thing.

"When we got into the Premiership, it was a watershed moment for us because we were able to retain the Academy boys that Robin Cowling was creating, who before, we were just losing at the age of 15 and 16 and they were going out of the county.

"Rob and I both share an ambition, apart from winning the Champions Cup, to field an all-West Country team one day, and the Academy is really producing some cracking young lads.

"If we can produce one or two boys from the Academy each year who go on into the first-team squad, it will be great."

So how do you celebrate winning the Premiership title if you are the chairman and chief executive of the successful team?

You get on a motorbike and go on a 5,000-mile round trip of Europe, of course!

That is what Rowe did with three friends the day after the Twickenham final.

"I have been around South America on my bike; I have done Canada; I have done Cape Town; I have been to Africa three or four times; which have all been

Exeter Chiefs head coach Rob Baxter with his son Jack and the Premiership trophy

fantastic, but I was running out of places to go to," explained Rowe, who rides a BMW Adventure.

"Over a cup of coffee one of the guys suggested going to Russia.

"It was quite a job to get our visas, but we went across Europe, up through Germany, Poland, Latvia, Lithuania, Estonia and then into Russia and up to St Petersburg. We then went on to Finland, Norway, Denmark and then back.

"It took us three weeks and it was about 5,000 miles. It was really good. I enjoyed the trip and I just enjoy the motorbiking, and we are now trying to think of where we can go next year!"

Then, within days of getting back to the UK, Rowe was the support driver as four directors from South West Communications Group, the main club sponsors of Exeter Chiefs, scaled the UK's highest three peaks to raise money for the Prince's Trust.

SW Comms' managing director Brian Lodge and fellow board members Jon Whiley, John Holdstock and Sean Doyle climbed Ben Nevis, Scafell Pike and Snowdon in 23 hours and 20 minutes to beat the required Three Peaks Challenge 24-hour deadline.

They also achieved this 29-mile, 3,064-metre feat on one of the hottest days of the year.

Rowe ensured the team stayed on track by driving between each peak and having drinks at the ready and the engine running at the foot of each mountain, and had a celebratory drink waiting for them as they completed the challenge.

Looking back on the season, Rowe said: "It was fantastic. Post-Christmas, I was fairly confident we could stay in the top four, but in any sport you are involved in, you need to have things drop into place.

"We should have progressed more in Europe, but would that have put us in a different place when we got to the end of the season?

"Were Saracens a bit off colour because they had gone through Europe? Maybe they were, and did that mean we stood a better chance of beating them? Maybe, I don't know, but things just fell into place for us."

So what now for Exeter Chiefs?

"We have just got to make sure we get better and improve year on year," said Rowe. "We can improve on winning the Premiership by winning it with a few more points, by winning the regular season and winning the Premiership, so there is a lot more we can do to improve, and I think we will."

Luke Cowan-Dickie asks his fellow Cornishman Jack Nowell to talk him through the try he created for him

Exeter Chiefs captain and matchwinner Gareth Steenson with the Aviva Premiership trophy

EXETER CHIEFS 2016-17
PLAYING SQUAD

DON ARMAND

Born:	Harare, Zimbabwe
DOB:	September 23, 1988
Position:	Back row/second row

Premiership appearances 2016-17: 17

Premiership tries 2016-17: 2

Champions Cup appearances 2016-17: 4

Champions Cup tries 2016-17: 0

Total appearances 2016-17: 21

Total tries 2016-17: 2

OLLIE ATKINS

Born:	Hobart, Australia
DOB:	August 12, 1988
Position:	Second row

Premiership appearances 2016-17: 8

Premiership tries 2016-17: 0

Champions Cup appearances 2016-17: 3

Champions Cup tries 2016-17: 0

Anglo-Welsh Cup appearances 2016-17: 5

Anglo Welsh Cup tries 2016-17: 0

Total appearances 2016-17: 16

Total tries 2016-17: 0

MAX BODILLY

Born:	Truro
DOB:	September 9, 1994
Position:	Full-back/winger/centre

Premiership appearances 2016-17: 1

Premiership tries 2016-17: 0

Champions Cup appearances 2016-17: 1

Champions Cup tries 2016-17: 0

Anglo-Welsh Cup appearances 2016-17: 6

Anglo Welsh Cup tries 2016-17: 2

Total appearances 2016-17: 8

Total tries 2016-17: 2

MICHELE CAMPAGNARO

Born:	Mirano, Italy
DOB:	March 13, 1993
Position:	Centre/wing

Premiership appearances 2016-17: 6

Premiership tries 2016-17: 2

Champions Cup appearances 2016-17: 4

Champions Cup tries 2016-17: 3

Anglo-Welsh Cup appearances 2016-17: 2

Anglo Welsh Cup tries 2016-17: 4

Total appearances 2016-17: 12

Total tries 2016-17: 9

JOSH CAULFIELD

Born:	Taunton
DOB:	June 9, 1997
Position:	Second row

Anglo-Welsh Cup appearances 2016-17: 1

Anglo Welsh Cup tries 2016-17: 0

Total appearances 2016-17: 1

Total tries 2016-17: 0

WILL CHUDLEY

Born:	Bedford
DOB:	March 17, 1994
Position:	Scrum-half

Premiership appearances 2016-17: 16

Premiership tries 2016-17: 5

Champions Cup appearances 2016-17: 2

Champions Cup tries 2016-17: 0

Anglo-Welsh Cup appearances 2016-17: 1

Anglo Welsh Cup tries 2016-17: 0

Total appearances 2016-17: 19

Total tries 2016-17: 5

LUKE COWAN-DICKIE

Born:	Truro
DOB:	June 20, 1993
Position:	Hooker

Premiership appearances 2016-17: 17

Premiership tries 2016-17: 6

Champions Cup appearances 2016-17: 4

Champions Cup tries 2016-17: 1

Total appearances 2016-17: 21

Total tries 2016-17: 7

DAVE DENNIS

Born:	Sydney, Australia
DOB:	January 10, 1986
Position:	Back row/second row

Premiership appearances 2016-17: 20

Premiership tries 2016-17: 0

Champions Cup appearances 2016-17: 5

Champions Cup tries 2016-17: 0

Total appearances 2016-17: 25

Total tries 2016-17: 0

OLLIE DEVOTO

Born:	Yeovil
DOB:	September 22, 1993
Position:	Centre/fly-half

Premiership appearances 2016-17: 22

Premiership tries 2016-17: 2

Champions Cup appearances 2016-17: 5

Champions Cup tries 2016-17: 1

Anglo-Welsh Cup appearances 2016-17: 2

Anglo Welsh Cup tries 2016-17: 0

Total appearances 2016-17: 29

Total tries 2016-17: 3

PHIL DOLLMAN

Born:	Caerphilly, Wales
DOB:	May 15, 1985
Position:	Full-back/centre

Premiership appearances 2016-17: 15

Premiership tries 2016-17: 1

Champions Cup appearances 2016-17: 3

Champions Cup tries 2016-17: 0

Anglo-Welsh Cup appearances 2016-17: 2

Anglo Welsh Cup tries 2016-17: 0

Total appearances 2016-17: 20

Total tries 2016-17: 1

DAVE EWERS

Born:	Harare, Zimbabwe
DOB:	November 3, 1990
Position:	Back row

Premiership appearances 2016-17: 5

Premiership tries 2016-17: 1

Champions Cup appearances 2016-17: 2

Champions Cup tries 2016-17: 0

Anglo-Welsh Cup appearances 2016-17: 3

Anglo Welsh Cup tries 2016-17: 0

Total appearances 2016-17: 10

Total tries 2016-17: 1

TOMAS FRANCIS

Born:	York
DOB:	April 27, 1993
Position:	Prop

Premiership appearances 2016-17: 11

Premiership tries 2016-17: 0

Champions Cup appearances 2016-17: 3

Champions Cup tries 2016-17: 0

Anglo-Welsh Cup appearances 2016-17: 1

Anglo Welsh Cup tries 2016-17: 0

Total appearances 2016-17: 15

Total tries 2016-17: 0

TOM HENDRICKSON

Born:	Nelson, New Zealand
DOB:	September 1, 1994
Position:	Centre

Anglo-Welsh Cup appearances 2016-17: 3

Anglo Welsh Cup tries 2016-17: 1

Total appearances 2016-17: 3

Total tries 2016-17: 1

ALEC HEPBURN

Born:	Perth, Australia
DOB:	March 3, 1993
Position:	Prop

Premiership appearances 2016-17: 5

Premiership tries 2016-17: 0

Total appearances 2016-17: 5

Total tries 2016-17: 0

JONNY HILL

Born:	Ludlow
DOB:	June 8, 1994
Position:	Second row

Premiership appearances 2016-17: 10

Premiership tries 2016-17: 0

Champions Cup appearances 2016-17: 4

Champions Cup tries 2016-17: 0

Anglo-Welsh Cup appearances 2016-17: 2

Anglo Welsh Cup tries 2016-17: 0

Total appearances 2016-17: 16

Total tries 2016-17: 0

SAM HILL

Born:	Exeter
DOB:	July 1, 1993
Position:	Centre

Premiership appearances 2016-17: 17

Premiership tries 2016-17: 2

Champions Cup appearances 2016-17: 3

Champions Cup tries 2016-17: 1

Anglo-Welsh Cup appearances 2016-17: 4

Anglo Welsh Cup tries 2016-17: 0

Total appearances 2016-17: 24

Total tries 2016-17: 3

GREG HOLMES

Born:	Warwick, Australia
DOB:	June 11, 1983
Position:	Prop

Premiership appearances 2016-17: 16

Premiership tries 2016-17: 0

Champions Cup appearances 2016-17: 4

Champions Cup tries 2016-17: 0

Anglo-Welsh Cup appearances 2016-17: 3

Anglo Welsh Cup tries 2016-17: 0

Total appearances 2016-17: 23

Total tries 2016-17: 0

WILL HOOLEY

Born:	Cambridge
DOB:	November 28, 1993
Position:	Fly-half

Premiership appearances 2016-17: 1

Premiership tries 2016-17: 0

Anglo-Welsh Cup appearances 2016-17: 5

Anglo Welsh Cup tries 2016-17: 0

Anglo-Welsh Cup points 2016-17: 2

Total appearances 2016-17: 6

Total tries 2016-17: 0

Total points 2016-17: 2

KAI HORSTMANN

Born:	Harare, Zimbabwe
DOB:	September 21, 1981
Position:	Back row

Premiership appearances 2016-17: 17

Premiership tries 2016-17: 2

Champions Cup appearances 2016-17: 6

Champions Cup tries 2016-17: 0

Total appearances 2016-17: 23

Total tries 2016-17: 2

JACK INNARD

Born:	Truro
DOB:	July 3, 1995
Position:	Hooker

Anglo-Welsh Cup appearances 2016-17: 3

Anglo Welsh Cup tries 2016-17: 1

Total appearances 2016-17: 3

Total tries 2016-17: 1

MATT JESS

Born:	Coventry
DOB:	April 4, 1984
Position:	Winger

Anglo-Welsh Cup appearances 2016-17: 4

Anglo Welsh Cup tries 2016-17: 0

Total appearances 2016-17: 4

Total tries 2016-17: 0

TOM JOHNSON

Born:	Dusseldorf, Germany
DOB:	July 16, 1982
Position:	Back row

Premiership appearances 2016-17: 2

Premiership tries 2016-17: 0

Champions Cup appearances 2016-17: 2

Champions Cup tries 2016-17: 0

Anglo-Welsh Cup appearances 2016-17: 4

Anglo Welsh Cup tries 2016-17: 1

Total appearances 2016-17: 8

Total tries 2016-17: 1

BILLY KEAST

Born:	Truro
DOB:	November 24, 1996
Position:	Prop

Anglo-Welsh Cup appearances 2016-17: 4

Anglo Welsh Cup tries 2016-17: 0

Total appearances 2016-17: 4

Total tries 2016-17: 0

TOM LAWDAY

Born:	Dorchester
DOB:	November 11, 1993
Position:	Back row

Anglo-Welsh Cup appearances 2016-17: 3

Anglo Welsh Cup tries 2016-17: 1

Total appearances 2016-17: 3

Total tries 2016-17: 1

MITCH LEES

Born:	Sydney, Australia
DOB:	October 12, 1988
Position:	Second row

Premiership appearances 2016-17: 20

Premiership tries 2016-17: 2

Champions Cup appearances 2016-17: 4

Champions Cup tries 2016-17: 0

Anglo-Welsh Cup appearances 2016-17: 1

Anglo Welsh Cup tries 2016-17: 1

Total appearances 2016-17: 25

Total tries 2016-17: 3

DAVE LEWIS

Born:	Manchester
DOB:	April 29, 1989
Position:	Scrum-half

Premiership appearances 2016-17: 7

Premiership tries 2016-17: 0

Champions Cup appearances 2016-17: 3

Champions Cup tries 2016-17: 0

Total appearances 2016-17: 10

Total tries 2016-17: 0

MORAY LOW

Born:	Torphins, Scotland
DOB:	November 28, 1984
Position:	Prop

Premiership appearances 2016-17: 2

Premiership tries 2016-17: 0

Champions Cup appearances 2016-17: 5

Champions Cup tries 2016-17: 0

Anglo-Welsh Cup appearances 2016-17: 4

Anglo Welsh Cup tries 2016-17: 0

Total appearances 2016-17: 11

Total tries 2016-17: 0

SHAUN MALTON

Born:	Durban, South Africa
DOB:	February 15, 1990
Position:	Hooker

Premiership appearances 2016-17: 6

Premiership tries 2016-17: 0

Champions Cup appearances 2016-17: 2

Champions Cup tries 2016-17: 0

Anglo-Welsh Cup appearances 2016-17: 6

Anglo Welsh Cup tries 2016-17: 3

Total appearances 2016-17: 14

Total tries 2016-17: 3

JACK MAUNDER

Born:	Exeter
DOB:	April 5, 1997
Position:	Scrum-half

Premiership appearances 2016-17: 13

Premiership tries 2016-17: 1

Champions Cup appearances 2016-17: 5

Champions Cup tries 2016-17: 1

Anglo-Welsh Cup appearances 2016-17: 3

Anglo Welsh Cup tries 2016-17: 0

Total appearances 2016-17: 21

Total tries 2016-17: 2

BEN MOON

Born:	Tiverton
DOB:	July 14, 1989
Position:	Prop

Premiership appearances 2016-17: 23

Premiership tries 2016-17: 1

Champions Cup appearances 2016-17: 3

Champions Cup tries 2016-17: 0

Anglo-Welsh Cup appearances 2016-17: 2

Anglo Welsh Cup tries 2016-17: 0

Total appearances 2016-17: 28

Total tries 2016-17: 1

WILL NORTON

Born:	Exeter
DOB:	March 28, 1993
Position:	Prop

Anglo-Welsh Cup appearances 2016-17: 1

Anglo Welsh Cup tries 2016-17: 0

Total appearances 2016-17: 1

Total tries 2016-17: 0

JACK NOWELL

Born:	Truro
DOB:	April 11, 1993
Position:	Winger/full-back

Premiership appearances 2016-17: 10

Premiership tries 2016-17: 4

Champions Cup appearances 2016-17: 3

Champions Cup tries 2016-17: 0

Total appearances 2016-17: 13

Total tries 2016-17: 4

JACK OWLETT

Born:	London
DOB:	February 2, 1995
Position:	Prop

Anglo-Welsh Cup appearances 2016-17: 3

Anglo Welsh Cup tries 2016-17: 0

Total appearances 2016-17: 3

Total tries 2016-17: 0

GEOFF PARLING

Born:	Stockton-on-Tees
DOB:	October 28, 1983
Position:	Second row

Premiership appearances 2016-17: 21

Premiership tries 2016-17: 1

Champions Cup appearances 2016-17: 3

Champions Cup tries 2016-17: 0

Anglo-Welsh Cup appearances 2016-17: 1

Anglo Welsh Cup tries 2016-17: 0

Total appearances 2016-17: 25

Total tries 2016-17: 1

CARL RIMMER

Born:	Banbury
DOB:	April 29, 1986
Position:	Prop

Premiership appearances 2016-17: 19

Premiership tries 2016-17: 1

Champions Cup appearances 2016-17: 4

Champions Cup tries 2016-17: 0

Anglo-Welsh Cup appearances 2016-17: 3

Anglo Welsh Cup tries 2016-17: 0

Total appearances 2016-17: 26

Total tries 2016-17: 1

JULIAN SALVI

Born:	Canberra, Australia
DOB:	October 9, 1985
Position:	Back row

Premiership appearances 2016-17: 8

Premiership tries 2016-17: 0

Champions Cup appearances 2016-17: 2

Champions Cup tries 2016-17: 0

Anglo-Welsh Cup appearances 2016-17: 3

Anglo Welsh Cup tries 2016-17: 1

Total appearances 2016-17: 13

Total tries 2016-17: 1

JAMES SHORT

Born:	Redhill
DOB:	October 15, 1989
Position:	Winger

Premiership appearances 2016-17: 18

Premiership tries 2016-17: 11

Champions Cup appearances 2016-17: 3

Champions Cup tries 2016-17: 1

Anglo-Welsh Cup appearances 2016-17: 3

Anglo Welsh Cup tries 2016-17: 2

Total appearances 2016-17: 24

Total tries 2016-17: 14

JOE SIMMONDS

Born:	Torquay
DOB:	December 19, 1996
Position:	Fly-half

Premiership appearances 2016-17: 6

Premiership tries 2016-17: 0

Premiership points 2016-17: 15

Champions Cup appearances 2016-17: 1

Champions Cup tries 2016-17: 0

Champions Cup points 2016-17: 2

Anglo-Welsh Cup appearances 2016-17: 6

Anglo Welsh Cup tries 2016-17: 0

Anglo-Welsh Cup points: 43

Total appearances 2016-17: 13

Total tries 2016-17: 0

Total points 2016-17: 60

SAM SIMMONDS

Born:	Torquay
DOB:	November 10, 1994
Position:	Back row

Premiership appearances 2016-17: 7

Premiership tries 2016-17: 3

Anglo-Welsh Cup appearances 2016-17: 5

Anglo Welsh Cup tries 2016-17: 4

Total appearances 2016-17: 12

Total tries 2016-17: 7

HARVEY SKINNER

Born:	Taunton
DOB:	December 31, 1997
Position:	Centre

Anglo-Welsh Cup appearances 2016-17: 1

Anglo Welsh Cup tries 2016-17: 0

Total appearances 2016-17: 1

Total tries 2016-17: 0

SAM SKINNER

Born:	Exeter
DOB:	January 31, 1995
Position:	Second row/back row

Premiership appearances 2016-17: 4

Premiership tries 2016-17: 1

Anglo-Welsh Cup appearances 2016-17: 3

Anglo Welsh Cup tries 2016-17: 0

Total appearances 2016-17: 7

Total tries 2016-17: 1

HENRY SLADE

Born:	Plymouth
DOB:	March 19, 1993
Position:	Fly-half/centre/full-back

Premiership appearances 2016-17: 17

Premiership tries 2016-17: 1

Premiership points 2016-17: 70

Champions Cup appearances 2016-17: 4

Champions Cup tries 2016-17: 0

Champions Cup points 2016-17: 10

Anglo-Welsh Cup appearances 2016-17: 1

Anglo Welsh Cup tries 2016-17: 1

Anglo-Welsh Cup points 2016-17: 5

Total appearances 2016-17: 22

Total tries 2016-17: 2

Total points 2016-17: 85

JOE SNOW

Born:	Taunton
DOB:	December 11, 1998
Position:	Scrum-half

Anglo-Welsh Cup appearances 2016-17: 2

Anglo Welsh Cup tries 2016-17: 0

Total appearances 2016-17: 2

Total tries 2016-17: 0

MARCUS STREET

Born:	Exeter
DOB:	February 6, 1999
Position:	Prop

Anglo-Welsh Cup appearances 2016-17: 1

Anglo Welsh Cup tries 2016-17: 0

Total appearances 2016-17: 1

Total tries 2016-17: 0

HARRY STRONG

Born:	Exeter
DOB:	June 12, 1997
Position:	Centre

Anglo-Welsh Cup appearances 2016-17: 2

Anglo Welsh Cup tries 2016-17: 0

Total appearances 2016-17: 2

Total tries 2016-17: 0

GARETH STEENSON

Born:	Dungannon, N Ireland
DOB:	April 5, 1984
Position:	Fly-half

Premiership appearances 2016-17: 21

Premiership tries 2016-17: 1

Premiership points 2016-17: 183

Champions Cup appearances 2016-17: 5

Champions Cup tries 2016-17: 0

Champions Cup points 2016-17: 33

Total appearances 2016-17: 26

Total tries 2016-17: 1

Total points 2016-17: 216

ELVIS TAIONE

Born:	Nuku'alofa, Tonga
DOB:	May 25, 1983
Position:	Hooker

Premiership appearances 2016-17: 2

Premiership tries 2016-17: 0

Anglo-Welsh Cup appearances 2016-17: 3

Anglo Welsh Cup tries 2016-17: 1

Total appearances 2016-17: 5

Total tries 2016-17: 1

HAYDN THOMAS

Born:	Birmingham
DOB:	September 17, 1982
Position:	Scrum-half

Anglo-Welsh Cup appearances 2016-17: 2

Anglo Welsh Cup tries 2016-17: 0

Total appearances 2016-17: 2

Total tries 2016-17: 0

STUART TOWNSEND

Born:	Torbay
DOB:	October 11, 1995
Position:	Scrum-half

Premiership appearances 2016-17: 11

Premiership tries 2016-17: 1

Champions Cup appearances 2016-17: 2

Champions Cup tries 2016-17: 0

Anglo-Welsh Cup appearances 2016-17: 4

Anglo Welsh Cup tries 2016-17: 2

Total appearances 2016-17: 17

Total tries 2016-17: 3

LACHIE TURNER

Born:	Sydney, Australia
DOB:	May 11, 1987
Position:	Full-back/winger

Premiership appearances 2016-17: 11

Premiership tries 2016-17: 4

Champions Cup appearances 2016-17: 3

Champions Cup tries 2016-17: 0

Anglo-Welsh Cup appearances 2016-17: 4

Anglo Welsh Cup tries 2016-17: 2

Total appearances 2016-17: 18

Total tries 2016-17: 6

THOMAS WALDROM

Born:	Lower Hutt, New Zealand
DOB:	April 28, 1983
Position:	No.8

Premiership appearances 2016-17: 20

Premiership tries 2016-17: 9

Champions Cup appearances 2016-17: 5

Champions Cup tries 2016-17: 3

Anglo-Welsh Cup appearances 2016-17: 1

Anglo Welsh Cup tries 2016-17: 0

Total appearances 2016-17: 26

Total tries 2016-17: 12

DAMIAN WELCH

Born:	Reading
DOB:	July 28, 1982
Position:	Second row

Premiership appearances 2016-17: 6

Premiership tries 2016-17: 1

Champions Cup appearances 2016-17: 2

Champions Cup tries 2016-17: 0

Anglo-Welsh Cup appearances 2016-17: 6

Anglo Welsh Cup tries 2016-17: 1

Total appearances 2016-17: 14

Total tries 2016-17: 2

BEN WHITE

Born:	Gosford, Australia
DOB:	December 19, 1986
Position:	Back row

Premiership appearances 2016-17: 3

Premiership tries 2016-17: 0

Anglo-Welsh Cup appearances 2016-17: 4

Anglo Welsh Cup tries 2016-17: 0

Total appearances 2016-17: 7

Total tries 2016-17: 0

IAN WHITTEN

Born:	Lisburn, Northern Ireland
DOB:	June 5, 1987
Position:	Centre

Premiership appearances 2016-17: 20

Premiership tries 2016-17: 6

Champions Cup appearances 2016-17: 5

Champions Cup tries 2016-17: 0

Anglo-Welsh Cup appearances 2016-17: 2

Anglo Welsh Cup tries 2016-17: 0

Total appearances 2016-17: 27

Total tries 2016-17: 6

HARRY WILLIAMS

Born:	London
DOB:	October 1, 1991
Position:	Prop

Premiership appearances 2016-17: 20

Premiership tries 2016-17: 1

Champions Cup appearances 2016-17: 5

Champions Cup tries 2016-17: 0

Anglo-Welsh Cup appearances 2016-17: 2

Anglo Welsh Cup tries 2016-17: 0

Total appearances 2016-17: 27

Total tries 2016-17: 1

OLLY WOODBURN

Born:	Bristol
DOB:	November 18, 1991
Position:	Winger

Premiership appearances 2016-17: 21

Premiership tries 2016-17: 10

Champions Cup appearances 2016-17: 5

Champions Cup tries 2016-17: 1

Anglo-Welsh Cup appearances 2016-17: 1

Anglo Welsh Cup tries 2016-17: 0

Total appearances 2016-17: 27

Total tries 2016-17: 11

JACK YEANDLE

Born:	Exeter
DOB:	December 22, 1989
Position:	Hooker

Premiership appearances 2016-17: 23

Premiership tries 2016-17: 2

Champions Cup appearances 2016-17: 5

Champions Cup tries 2016-17: 0

Total appearances 2016-17: 28

Total tries 2016-17: 2

A VERY SPECIAL JOURNEY

By Nigel Walrond

IT has been a real treat covering Exeter Chiefs for *BBC Radio Devon* for the past 14 years.

I was delighted when I was asked by the then sports editor Richard Green if I would be interested in taking on the job as Alan Mackie was standing down.

I was born and brought up in Plymouth, and Beacon Park was my regular haunt on a Saturday afternoon as a youngster. The derby matches with Exeter were always memorable occasions (in those days, before television match officials and citing officers, it was always a miracle if both sides ended the game with 15 players still on the pitch!).

However, whenever my dad took the family on a weekend visit up to his mum and dad, who lived in Velwell Road on the edge of Exeter city centre, it did not need too much persuasion to get him to take me to the County Ground.

I always remember him shouting out: "Come on the Chiefs!". It was just plain old Exeter Rugby Club in those days, but the first teams of many clubs were known as the Chiefs, with Extras or United the moniker given to clubs' second, and even third, XV's.

When the club went semi-professional, the name was changed to Exeter Chiefs as part of a rebranding in 1999, and I think my dad was very approving of that.

When I started working as a freelance for *Radio Devon*, I already knew plenty about the club, as I had been covering South West rugby for 11 years up to that point for either the *Western Morning News, Evening Herald* or *Sunday Independent*, bar a two-year gap in the early 2000s, when I worked for the *BBC'S* Grandstand and Match of the Day programmes, and also for *Sky Sports*.

In 2004, you could sense it was a club really going places, with plans for a new stadium at Sandy Park in the pipeline and ambitions to one day reach the Premiership, but you would never have dreamt the rise would be so meteoric.

My new role could not have got off to a better start, with Exeter beating Manchester 85-6 – a club record score. Club officials asked me if I could come back again!

Photo above: BBC Radio Devon commentary team Nigel Walrond and John Lockyer on duty at Twickenham
Photo top right: BBC Radio Devon commentator Nigel Walrond and summariser John Lockyer working at Sandy Park

The only problem was condensing so many scorers into a three-minute radio report!

Tony Yapp contributed 30 points, Richard Baxter scored his 50th try on his 150th league appearance for the club, and it was a very happy Yappy and director of rugby Ian Bremner that I interviewed after the game.

Reporting on the Chiefs quickly developed into commentating on their matches, and I will never forget my first crack at that.

Radio Devon were taking live commentary from Exeter City's game at Southend United, but the line went down, and they crossed to me and asked me to commentate on my match until they had restored the link.

The problem was Exeter were playing Otley on a day when the heavens had opened, the County Ground was a sea of mud, and it was impossible to tell one set of players from another. The shirts were so indistinguishable that you had players passing to the opposition. Talk about being thrown in at the deep end!

However, every game after that seemed easy in comparison, and it was not long before *Radio Devon* were providing commentary on all of Exeter's home and away games, and I was joined by John Lockyer, who has been a fantastic summariser, and friend to me, over many years now.

During the past 14 years, I have also continued to cover the club for many local and national newspapers, including the *Daily* and *Sunday Telegraph* in recent seasons.

I have been so lucky to be able to follow a club that has constantly been on the rise over the past decade or so. It has enabled me to visit some fabulous European cities with the Chiefs, and commentate from some great venues – and those help make up for the Friday night games in sub-zero temperatures at places like Kingston Park in Newcastle or Sale's AJ Bell Stadium.

I have also been so fortunate to have someone as excellent to deal with as Rob Baxter, who has that incredible ability to so lucidly give his thoughts on a game within moments of it finishing.

I still find it hard to believe that the team I started commentating on all those years ago at a dilapidated County Ground lifted the Premiership trophy in May, though writing this book has helped it to sink in.

Thanks Chiefs, it has been a real blast, and I am looking forward to where you are going to take me next on this very special journey.

The 'Originals': the six members of Exeter's Premiership-winning squad who won the Championship with the Chiefs in 2010, at the Exeter Guildhall reception to celebrate the title triumph. From left to right: Tom Johnson, Ben Moon, Matt Jess, Haydn Thomas, Phil Dollman and Gareth Steenson